S0-ARX-782

Time and a Ticket

Time and a Ticket

Peter Benchley

HOUGHTON MIFFLIN COMPANY BOSTON
THE RIVERSIDE PRESS CAMBRIDGE
1964

First Printing

The Riverside Press
Cambridge Massachusetts
Printed in the U.S.A.

For My Parents
Tutto per Tutti gli Sport

Foreword

When, on June 15, 1961, Harvard's President Pusey welcomed me into "the society of educated men," I was terrified. For the first time in my life I was a free agent, and the sudden disappearance of the security of school life—the discipline, the small community, and the minor, predictable worries—left me feeling unprotected and alone. The cockiness of the college student left me, and I felt unqualified to face the world on adult terms. Instinct urged me to flee back to the bosom of academe and apply to graduate school.

But I was more fortunate than many of my classmates, for I was to be granted a reprieve from the military and from the necessity of making money. Since I had been unable to secure one of Harvard's many traveling fellowships, my parents and I worked out our own grant, whereby they would support me for a given length of time, and when that money ran out, I would support myself. I could go as far and stay as long as my finances would permit.

After some consideration, a friend, Charles Ravenel, and I decided to go around the world. Ravenel had received a grant from Corning Glass about equal to my Benchley Family Fellowship, and we thought we should take advantage of the chance to travel so extensively, a chance we would most probably not have again. The thought of the dark robes of Cambridge and the glass slivers on the tops of the walls at Oxford depressed us, while names like Kuala Lumpur, Rawalpindi, and Sarawak chimed of adventures unrecorded in Harvard Yard.

I spent the summer and fall in Europe, mostly in Paris, and on the tenth of February met Charlie in Cairo. From Egypt we traveled in Jordan, Israel, Iran, Pakistan, India, Ceylon, Singapore, Malaya, Thailand, Hong Kong, and Japan. In late April we touched down in Honolulu, somehow surviving what the Pan American pilot laughingly described as a "simulated bombing run" from thirty-three thousand feet.

There was no specific purpose to the trip, and this was a great boon. I had no mission, and therefore no limitations. I could look, I could listen, I could see what and whom I wished when I wished, and I could spend as much or as little time in a place as I chose. I knew I could not be as thorough or perceptive an observer as Alsop or Gunther, but I had one thing that they could no longer have: an untutored, and thus open, outlook on the world. I knew so little, had so much to learn, that everything—political, economic, social—could prove new and fascinating to me.

I began the trip with few opinions of my own. It is an

unsettling fact that American youth are wretchedly informed about their own nation's problems, not to mention those of the world. Though my ignorance occasionally acted to my advantage, in letting me form my own opinions, I was soon *forced* to study, to become aware, in order to gain an equal footing with the people I talked to. And, as will happen with study, the more I read, the more I learned; and the more I learned, the more it interested me.

I was fortunate in having opportunities to meet many people unavailable to most tourists. Charlie had contacts with business and government men through Corning Glass, the Harvard Business School, and the Eisenhower Exchange Fellowship program (through one such contact we met Prime Minister Nehru), some friends of mine were at various foreign service posts, and Charlie carried a letter of introduction from the White House, which made it possible for us to talk to officers in American embassies around the world. Also, since we were not traveling with a group, we were foreigners, and obviously so, but we were not a tightly knit American unit whose members clustered, as in a swarm, around a guide. Many times we were accosted in railroad stations, on streets, in restaurants, by people who wanted to practice their English or to argue a political idea, or who were simply curious about Americans.

One night in particular, we were waiting for a train on the station platform in Jaipur, India, en route southwest to Ahmedabad, a dusty, plains-country industrial town. The platform was packed. Elegantly turbaned Sikhs held sleeping babies in their big hands, old women squatted on their heels and peeled tangerines or chewed dark red betel and spat professionally over the edge of the platform. Whole families lay sleeping on their luggage, and always there was the noise of the food and magazine vendors hawking their wares in long, musical Hindi tones. The atmosphere was, above all, one of patience and calm. No one complained, no one spoke sharply to anyone else, no one raised his voice. Already the train was forty minutes late.

Charlie and I edged our way along the platform until we found enough space to set our bags down. A loudspeaker shrieked, first in Hindi, then in English, that the train would be delayed another hour, and Charlie got a book from his suitcase and sat down to read. I saw an empty spot a few feet away, located a frayed copy of *Borstal Boy* that had sunk into the lining of my raincoat, and curled up next to a steel post.

I read for a while, and then fell asleep. Suddenly I had the feeling that someone was looking at me. I was neither surprised nor uneasy, for Americans are great curiosities in some parts of India, and people often squat down and stare at you for a few minutes, until they get bored and realize that you're not going to do magic for them or exhude blue fire from your ears as you breathe. I looked up, and standing in front of me was a short, thin young man dressed, like most Indian men, entirely in white. He had long black hair and bad teeth, which he showed through a nervous smile. I nodded, assuming that he would say nothing, and went back to Brendan Behan.

"What do you in America think about Communism?" he said suddenly.

The question startled me. "That's like saying 'What do you think about God?' isn't it? It's a little broad."

"All right, do you like Communism, you in America?"

"No."

"I am a Communist," he said, proudly. And then, to make sure I wouldn't hedge on an argument, he said, "The Russians are good people, better than anybody."

"Why is that?"

"They gave us a steel mill."

"Well, the Americans gave you two and a half billion dollars *and* a steel mill," I said.

"Yes, but the Americans are not good people."

"Why not?"

"They criticized us on Goa."

"I see. Look, if you like the Russians only because they gave you a steel mill, from your standpoint one steel mill should equal one unit of goodness, right?"

"Yes."

"But we gave you a steel mill and two and a half billion dollars, so that's two units, minus one unit to make up for the unit of badness in criticizing you on Goa, which leaves us one unit, or just as much as the Russians."

He was, understandably, confused. "No," he said. "The Russians are good people. The Americans are not good people."

Just then the train arrived, and as it slowed and doors were flung open and bags tossed out through compartment windows, I turned to the young man and said, "You're the most dangerous kind of Communist there is."

He smiled, showing me three black teeth. "What kind is that?" There was a cockiness in his voice.

"The stupid kind," I said, and got on the train. I sat down and looked out the window, and he was standing still, his mouth hanging slightly ajar as if he were looking for something to say. I could feel no sense of victory in shutting him up, for it was a cheap victory and could have done no good. But he *was* the stupid kind, the unquestioning, follow-the-leader kind, and that *is* the most dangerous kind, and the whole thought depressed me.

If we had been with a group, we would not have been able

to experience this type of opposition, would probably never have become aware of this aspect of Communism. And yet all throughout the East, these are the people to worry about —the ones who will never know another way, who are indoctrinated early and completely, and who have been taught never to question anything. They are happy in their beliefs, for they have nary a doubt. But it is a blind, dulling security. While Americans and British and French can argue principles back and forth, every day more young people, from East Germany to North Korea to Cuba, are being molded and hardened into beings incapable of independent thought.

On my return, it was perfectly natural for me to try to analyze what I had "gotten out of" the trip. I was unable to judge if there had been any basic changes in me—such changes occur slowly and subtly, and are not, really, for one to analyze in oneself. Having been there, I knew for certain that Karachi is not a town in New Jersey. I had developed an interest in, and an awareness of, politics and international goings-on, which a year earlier would have bored me to distraction. And I had come to realize, not without awe, the magnitude and complexity of even the apparently most insignificant of the world's problems. I can't say that the realization made me gloriously broad-minded, but it did make me want to try to understand, to explore more than the one or two obvious sides of a problem.

But most important, I think I learned a great deal more about America by being away from it than I could ever have learned by staying home. I heard people in the NATO countries curse America, and people in neutral countries praise us to the skies. I had lessons in American history from Malayans, learned about our support of the Balfour Declaration from a bitter Arab and a successful Jew, and heard of

Arthur Miller's remarriage from a Pakistani. And I saw Americans away from home, Americans stripped of domestic security yet seething with national pride, Americans representing not so much the United States as the Ku Klux Klan, and Americans making friends for America by slogging through miles of mud and sand to help a farmer grow watermelons.

I could come to no general conclusions about the places I saw. The problems, even on the level that I saw them, defied generalization. They vary not only from country to country, but from district to district and town to town. What the region produces, who its leaders are, what its soil is like, what religion the people profess, these and innumerable other factors all determine what can or should be done. I developed opinions on particular situations, and with those that I could not form an opinion on, I tried to lard my confusion with as much knowledge as possible.

It is a world I look forward to with apprehension, gingerly placing an exploratory toe in its icy waters. But it is a world that I consider myself fortunate to have seen at an age when I could still laugh at some of it, be terrified by more of it, and learn from it all.

Time and a Ticket

1

THE weather in Paris was perfect. It was early July, before
the season of shimmering heat that drives Parisians to the
country in August, and as we flew over the city, descending
slowly toward the runway at Orly, I could see the yellow
reflections of the sun on the white buildings along the Seine.

When I had collected my bags from customs, I strapped
them to the top of one of the square black Citroën taxis and
stepped inside. Though the air was cool, I was dressed for
an Arctic winter, so I was sweating. I rolled the windows all
the way down. As the driver, a heavyset old man with deep
rivers of wrinkles in his rough face, got in, he looked at
the windows and then glared at me. He wrenched the car
into gear, and we lurched down the ramp.

I was lying back, eyes closed, basking in the strong breeze, when I heard the driver muttering to himself. I opened my eyes and saw that he was hunched down in his seat, a muffler wrapped twice around his neck.

"What's the matter?" I said.

"Are you a bear from the North Pole?"

"No. Why?"

"Why must you have the windows open so far?"

"I was hot."

"It is not healthy," he said.

"Why not?"

"They should not be open like that. You should have them all open only a crack. That way one gets a cross draft, but a gentle one, and no one gets a chill."

"As you wish," I said, and I rolled the windows most of the way up.

"Thank you," he said, sitting straight in his seat. "It is my liver, you see. One cannot be too careful about one's liver."

I had been given the name of a hotel near St. Germain des Prés. It was a small hotel, I had been told, cheap but clean, and as the taxi turned off the Boulevard St. Germain and climbed the cobblestones on the Rue Monsieur le Prince, the picture I had created in my mind of what the hotel would be like suddenly came true. It nestled between a café and a tobacconist off a small square. The streets nearby were narrow and completely without plan—some were one-way up the first half, one-way down the second half. The stores and cafés were small and dark, and people sat at tiny round tables in the sun, drinking Perrier and Coca-Cola. Above an old wooden door hung a sign, "Hôtel St. Paul."

"You are very lucky," said the concierge. She was a big woman, with hair that stuck straight out from either side of her head and a broad, friendly smile. "I have but one empty room. But it is one of the biggest rooms in the hotel, and it is, *naturellement,* one of the most expensive."

I asked how much it was.

"Thirteen hundred francs," she said. Thirteen new francs, two dollars and sixty cents a day.

I said I would take it.

"You will be very happy. The room has three beds and two windows."

Indeed, the room had three beds—two doubles and a single, set across the room from each other on a floor that sloped steeply to the right. I mentioned the angle of the floor.

"C'est rigolo, non?" she said. "One must get used to the room before one comes in late at night having had too much to drink." She laughed and went out.

I kicked my shoes off and jumped onto the bigger of the two double beds. I was ecstatic about being in Paris again, but at the same time apprehensive about having *no* responsibilities, nothing I *had* to do, nowhere I *had* to go, no one to whom I *had* to answer. Then I began to think that having no responsibilities really meant that I did have one great responsibility, a responsibility to myself to do something, to learn, to meet people, to *create* responsibilities. It was all too confusing, and I went to sleep.

I had chosen Paris as the stepping-off place and, if there was to be such, the home base for the trip for a number of reasons. It was the only city in Europe that I knew at all. I had spent some time there in 1957, and I felt, if not completely at home, at least not completely lost. I could handle the language without being embarrassed, although my

prowess was mostly in accent and almost not at all in grammar. My plans for the summer were indefinite: I might go
here, I might go there, I might go alone, I might go with
someone, I might even (my recurring dream of glory) be
discovered by a beautiful lady who lived in a château and
taken as her lover for the summer.

Paris is a fine place to wait while making up one's mind
—about anything. I was waiting there trying to decide
where to go. During the war, the French army waited there
so long trying to settle on a course of action that they found
themselves occupied. German officers waited there trying to
decide where the Allies would land, and they found themselves invaded. Even in Caesar's time, armies would stop in
the city, then known as Lutèce, to get their breaths and decide whom to conquer next.

The life is conducive to leisurely pondering, especially
in the summer. I would get up early and have breakfast at
a small café on the Odéon. I would walk down St. Germain
and cross the river by the Assemblée Nationale, stopping to
lean on the rail of the bridge and gaze at the boats and barges
that eased their way upriver. On the right bank, each day
I would try a different method of crossing the perilous Place
de la Concorde, where the traffic speeds around in circles
and peels off into the many streets that lead off it. I walked
up the Grands Boulevards, past the Madeleine, and stopped
at the Café de la Paix to have a glass of orange juice and
stare at the people who were staring at the people who were
staring at the people—whole lives have been spent at this
Parisian sport of people watching. Sometimes, if I was feeling energetic, I walked all the way to Montmartre and stood
on the balcony by Sacré Coeur, looking down on all of Paris.
Otherwise, I walked down the Rue de Rivoli or by the

river's edge and over the bridge to the Ile St. Louis, where
one can spend days poking around in seventeenth and
eighteenth century courtyards. I had lunch in one of the
cafés on the Boulevard St. Michel. If I had any business to
attend to, such as filling out the myriad papers that accom-
pany the purchase of a car, I did that in the afternoon. If
not, I bought a book and sat for hours at a sidewalk table,
nursing one drink. Or I stopped by at the American Express
to see if I had any mail or if any of the people I was half
expecting had arrived.

At night, if I was not supping with one of the few people
I knew in Paris, I ate at one of the fine, inexpensive restaurants on St. Germain. After dinner I walked some more,
looking at the parties that overflowed the restaurants, pouring glass-clutching people into the streets, or I bought a paper
and sat at the Deux Magots and drank brandy, not reading
so much as listening to the conversations around me. On
such a night I rarely went to bed after midnight.

One night, I was walking up Rue Monsieur le Prince toward the St. Paul, yawning and stretching and luxuriating
in the warm air, when I was suddenly clasped on both shoulders by two huge hands.

"You're a dead man," said a voice, and for a moment I
believed him. Then I was spun around and found myself
staring into the face of an old friend, Bob Resky, with whom
I had made vague plans about possibly touring Europe.

Resky is not a big man, under six feet and small-boned.
Like myself, he was jumped a grade in grammar school and
was graduated from Harvard at twenty. Unlike myself, however, he skipped a grade because he was brighter than his
classmates. I was just bigger. Although he is an excellent
swimmer and an enthusiastic wrestler, he has—again like

myself—an interest in the more sedentary pleasures. He has an open, almost effusive manner with people he likes, and when he assumes an ultrasophisticated, blasé air, it is more to amuse himself than to create a serious impression. He has a quick mind and, when he wants to use it, a savage, biting tongue.

Bob was going to be in Paris for four or five days before going to Zurich for a week to see his girl, and since he had not yet taken a room, I put him in one of my two extra beds, thereby lowering the price of the room to $1.30 per person per day. We settled our plans immediately: as soon as he returned from Zurich, we would start for Denmark in the car I was in the process of obtaining, a Peugeot 403. We would stop in Holland, where he knew some people who, he said, would be glad to put us up. After Denmark, we would go wherever we felt like going.

When Bob had hung up his clothes, we decided that since the night was, if not exactly young, at least no more than middle-aged, we would go up to Pigalle and have a drink and look around and listen to the raucous cries of the multitudes of importunate prostitutes.

Even now, Pigalle enjoys great notoriety all over the world. Just after the war, it was known to American soldiers as Pig-Alley, where any and all pleasures, of the flesh, of the taste, and of the eye, could be had for a nominal fee. For the man who was weary of active sex, there were the *exhibitions,* private showings, by from one to five people, of every conceivable sexual diversion. For the less affluent, there were the movies, the "skin fliks," or a tour through one of the brothels that had windows or glass doors in certain rooms, affording the curious visitor a few vicarious thrills.

Although the law has put a stop to some of the more extreme activities in Pigalle, a great deal still goes on, some

within, some beyond the law. And the girls, though theoretically prohibited from flaunting their wares on the side-
walks, manage to advertise effectively. Bob and I wandered
around, fascinated by the innumerable propositions, threats,
cajoleries, and tales of family woe.

"Hey, boy," said a dirty, wizened old man, "you wan' see
feelthy pictures?"

"I take my own," said Bob.

As we walked out of a small side street onto one of the
broad avenues, we noticed a large, noisy crowd gathered
around a café. The people were all swarthy, and most of
them sported black mustaches.

"Algerians," I said. "I think we'd better steer clear."

"Wait a minute," said Bob. "Maybe there'll be some
action."

Suddenly we heard the braying eee-yaaww siren of a police
wagon, and a black truck careened around the corner and
screeched to a stop. Policemen poured out of the back of the
truck, swinging their lead-weighted capes into the crowd,
pushing the people away with the muzzles of their submachine guns.

When the crowd had moved away, one man stood alone
by a table. He was a tall man, dark-skinned and very erect.
A policeman motioned to him to put up his hands. Slowly,
with a deliberateness that was more mockery than obedience,
he raised his hands. The policeman lifted the man's jacket
and went quickly over his body checking for weapons. The
man began to drop his hands.

"Keep them there!" snapped the cop.

"Ah, *ta gueule*," said the man, more bored than angry.

The words were not out of his mouth before a cop kicked
him from behind. He sprawled forward on the street. Two
policemen grabbed his arms and dragged him toward the

truck while the others kept the crowd at bay with their
guns. They threw the man into the truck, and all the policemen piled in after him. The driver started the engine. A
policeman slammed the tailgate, sat down, slid the bolt on
his machine gun, and pointed it at the crowd as the truck
jumped to a start and sped away, its siren screaming a warning to everyone on the street.

Feeling that he had had enough "action" for the time being, Bob left Paris for Zurich on July 13, purposely avoiding
the holocaust that he knew Bastille Day would produce. He
was not alone. For days before the 14th, the highways leading out of Paris were jammed, the trains full, and airplane
reservations almost impossible to obtain.

The French run from Paris on the anniversary of the
French Revolution the way Americans run from the city on
Labor Day. But they are not running *to* something, to a
quiet weekend in the country or a gay party in the Loire
valley, as much as they are running away—from the mad-
house that Paris becomes on Bastille Day.

All day the city was alive with noise. Before, during, and
after the parade up the Champs Elysées, people threw fire-
crackers and cherry bombs, exploded rockets, smashed glasses,
and sang in the streets. I had dined with some friends, and
after dinner we went to the Ile de la Cité to watch the fireworks display over the Seine. Launching stations had been
set up on both sides of the river, and blue and red and yellow
rockets arched over the water and exploded above Notre
Dame. When the display was over, five of us climbed into
an open car and began the drive up the Champs to Fouquet's,
the venerable café where we were going to have a Bastille
Day drink.

Evidently, everyone else in Paris had the same idea. The jam started on the lower end of the Rue de Rivoli and extended all the way up to the Arc de Triomphe. We were caught in the middle of it, and could go neither forward nor back nor to either side.

I was sitting up on top of the back seat when someone screamed "Look out!" I ducked as a cherry bomb flew by my head and exploded on the hood of the car next to us. "Encore un!" said a girl sitting with me, and I looked helplessly at the red ball as it came straight down toward the open car. The driver hit it away with his hat, screaming, "Salaud! Oh! la vache. Salaud!" The bomb exploded beside the car and seared the paint. The two boys who stood on the sidewalk throwing the bombs roared with laughter. The driver started to get out of the car, but just then the traffic began to move and he sat back in his seat.

Twenty minutes later we reached the bottom of the Champs Elysées, having traveled some three hundred yards. People were standing on the tops of cars, screaming at one another. Girls were perched prettily on the hoods, smiling at everyone. Then, as a gesture of anger and frustration, one man blew his horn. It was a short beep, and not very loud, but that was unimportant. The law had been broken, someone had set the precedent, and suddenly, almost on cue, everyone blew his horn, until the skein of traffic was snarling and barking and whining at itself in an orgy of futile French passion.

It took us an hour and three-quarters to get to Fouquet's. A time-distance comparison later indicated that we might have made it in less time had we rolled eggs up the Rue de Rivoli with our noses.

*   *   *

When we left Fouquet's, I decided not to brave the traffic
on the Champs Elysées again. I convinced the girl who was
with me, Carol Harper, whom I had known slightly in college, that we could make better time on the subway, and we
threaded our way through the crowds on the street to the
nearest Métro station.

By midnight, most of the stations are empty. The *clochards*
have been poked and awakened and sent on their way, and
the ticket puncher slumps in her booth and either dozes or
stares dreamily at the black mouth of the tunnel. Every
twenty or thirty minutes, a train grinds and shrieks and
bangs out of the blackness to a stop, opens one, maybe two,
of its sliding doors, and disgorges a few people who shuffle
down the platform and climb the stairs one by one, pulling
on the railing with each step. When the train has gone, the
ticket puncher is alone again, with no one to talk to except
the seductive blond girls who grin down from the bra ads
and whisper their message of love.

Carol and I got off at the Avenue Kléber station, and I
took her arm as we started up the stairs. We turned right
at the landing which joins the stairways from either side of
the tracks into one bank of twenty steps leading to the street
level. Suddenly Carol stopped. Her eyes widened and her
mouth opened, and she pointed at the third stair. There,
nestled against the wall, was a red metal can with rounded
edges. I had never seen anything like it.

Carol finally managed to speak. "What is it?" she said.

"It's probably a bomb," I said, only half joking. "We'd
better get past it. Come on." I nudged her forward.

"No!" she said, yanking her arm away. "I bet it is a bomb.
I—"

Before she could finish the sentence, the swinging doors
at the top of the stairs flew open and five policemen rushed

down toward us. Their submachine guns bounced wildly on
their hips. Carol grabbed my shoulders and backed against
the wall, shielding herself from the object.

The policemen gathered around the can. Four of them
pointed their guns at it, and the fifth, the youngest-looking,
stood a few steps above it, an arm half raised in uncertain
defense. For a moment they said nothing, but stood crouched
at the ready with the muzzles of their guns focused on the
can.

"Plastique?" said one.

"You think?" said another.

"How do you know?" said a third.

"Je ne sais pas, moi," said the first. "I was just asking."

"And you, what do you think?" said a fourth cop to the
young one.

"I don't like it," he said, moving up another step.

"I didn't ask if you liked it. It's all the same to me if you
like it or don't. But what do you think it *is?"*

There was no reply.

The fourth policeman started to speak again, then decided
against it. He leaned toward the can with one finger outstretched. I started to edge up the stairs.

"No!" snapped Carol. "Don't move any closer." She held
my shoulders tighter. I felt my hands go clammy, and sweat
ran into my eyes. I thought of diving for the lower staircase
and the protection of the corner, but the finger was already
too close to the can. We should have run immediately we
saw it, but it was a little late to think of that now.

When the finger was no more than half an inch away from
the can, the policeman stopped. He turned his head and
smiled nervously at the barrel of a machine gun pointed at
his hand. Then, very gently, he touched the object. He
jerked his finger away and put it to his tongue.

"What does it taste like?"

"Strawberry or raspberry?" said the young one, with a choked laugh.

"It is," said the policeman momentously, "painted metal."

"Bravo. But what in the name of God *is* it?"

"How should I know?"

"You tasted it."

"So what does that prove?"

"Then why did you taste it?"

"Why not?"

"Now listen . . ."

Slowly, I maneuvered Carol and myself down around the corner.

"Now what?" she said when we had the corner between us and the can.

"We'd better go down to the bottom."

"Why?"

"If it is a bomb, and if it does go off, the ricochets would get us here."

"We'll have to stay down there all night?"

"No. They'll do something about it soon. Even if they don't, we can take the subway to the next stop."

"You're sure, are you?" she said. "Maybe they've stopped running."

"Look, if you'd gone up with me in the first place, we'd be out of here and home having a drink."

"Oh, shut up!"

"*Ta gueule.*"

"What does that mean?"

"Never mind."

"You know, sometimes you—"

"Ssshh! They're deciding." I knelt down and peeked around the corner. The policemen were arguing.

"Well, *some*body has to do it," said the one who had tasted the metal.

"Then do it," said one of the others.

"I already touched it," he said. "It's up to someone else."

"Why don't you defuse it?"

"Defuse it, *mon cul!* It probably doesn't even have a fuse."

"Then why hasn't it gone off?"

"Maybe it isn't a bomb."

"So pick it up and carry it, then."

"You pick it up," said the first policeman. "I outrank you."

They fell silent. Then, as if the thought occurred to all of them at once, the four who were pointing their guns at the can looked at the youngest, who still had his arms raised.

The one who spoke, spoke very softly. "C'est á toi, mon petit," he said. "It's up to you."

The young man looked horrified. "Moi! Pourquoi moi?"

"Because you are the youngest," said the policeman, with the gentleness of an understanding parent.

The young man looked from one pair of eyes to the next, but he found no encouragement. He walked slowly down the steps and stood over the object. Desperately, he turned around and tried to speak, but all he could utter was a strangled *"Mais . . ."* He bent down and cupped his hands. Gingerly, he lifted the can and held it at arm's length, turning his head to the side. The four other policemen raised their guns, and the troop started up the stairs.

Carol and I waited for the explosion. We heard a door slam, an engine start, and a truck drive away. Then, almost as an afterthought, the loud eee-yaw, eee-yaw of the siren began, and the sound echoed down into the station with an eerie hollowness.

2

THE day before Bob returned from Zurich, I picked up my car. Among the "optional extras" on French cars are such frivolities as an ignition key, an ignition lock, and a side mirror, so I spent hours having these devices installed, trying the while to determine how the French keep their cars from being stolen. I finally concluded that they don't care.

The weather was still fine, and I decided to give Peugeot her maiden voyage on a one-day trip to the beaches at Normandy.

To my generation, World War II is a strange and distant phenomenon. Our families were in the war, and some of us lost an uncle or cousin or even a father. But at the age of three or four or five, one's interest is almost exclusively in oneself, and the loss was not staggering. We didn't compre-

hend it. We cried only because Mother was crying. We had
a sense only that something was wrong. When Mother put it
right by smiling bravely, everything was okay. Daddy was
a stranger. When he came home and made Mother happy,
we were probably jealous because he was taking her attention away from us. When he left and made her cry, we probably hated him for hurting her. Not the most sympathetic
of characters to a three-year-old.

All our familiarity with the war has come from books
and movies. We can't look on it as truly horrible, because
all the movies made it romantic. All sergeants either looked
like John Wayne or were killed before the picture ended.
Some Americans died, sure, but they died performing such
acts of bravery that they must have died happy. All nurses
were beautiful, and as ghastly as Guadalcanal was, there was
always a nurse to be found somewhere. She would be trying
to forget, and thus she would be cold and brave and silent.
But she could be won, just like everything else.

To us, the war is not real. And so, as I drove north from
Paris, I tried to forget John Wayne and to concentrate on
what facts I actually knew about the invasion of June 6, 1944.
I remembered Cornelius Ryan's *The Longest Day,* the de-
scriptions of the men riding across the channel, the needless
and absurd drownings and crashes and bunglings, the heavy
losses in the first wave. Still, the losses meant nothing to
me. They were statistics. Five thousand killed here, five
thousand there, but five thousand whats? Five thousand
names, none of which affected me in the slightest.

The cemetery sits high on the cliffs. The graves are arranged in neat rows, crosses and stars of David three or four
feet apart. All the monuments are the same—clean, white
stones—and the inscriptions are uniformly simple—name

(when known), rank, dates of birth and death. It is a military cemetery, and as such it is orderly and beautifully kept.

I first began to realize what I was seeing as I walked between the rows of graves and noticed the dates of death. It was not like a regular cemetery; there were no people here from 1904, 1915, 1935. There were no old men. There were no women. "June 6, 1944; June 6, 1944; June 6, 1944; June 7, 1944; July 25, 1944; June 6, 1944; June 6, 1944; June 8, 1944; July 3, 1944; June 6, 1944." It didn't seem possible that all these lives could have stopped at once, that one day could have extinguished so many plans and hopes. The war began to mean something more than statistics.

But it was not until I stood on the edge of the cliff that I felt any connection between the crosses in the cemetery and the war itself. The sky was gray, and a brisk wind blew off the channel, as it had blown seventeen years before. Two landing barges lay on the beach, rusted and partly covered by sand. German obstacles stuck out of the choppy water, grotesque bits of twisted steel that could sink a small boat or impale a man. On the 6th of June, 1944, the men who lay not ten yards behind me had crouched in their boats not a hundred yards in front of me and tried to put the thought of death from their minds. They were seasick and homesick and frightsick, but they could not believe that they were going to die. It might be the other guy, might be the lieutenant or the sergeant or even a buddy, but never oneself. They landed in front of me and fought below me and died, many of them, where I stood, and now they lay behind me. It was all there, the whole story from start to finish.

For the first time in my life, I, only a year or two away from being a war baby, understood that a war—a real, honest-to-God war—had taken place. . . .

Bob returned from Zurich on July 18, starry-eyed and not looking forward to being away from his young lady. We spent one last sodden evening on the town, and at eight o'clock the following morning set out for Amsterdam.

The route from Paris to Amsterdam crosses a large part of Belgium, and the scenery is nothing short of dingy. Dark, characterless red brick houses line the road through every small town. The road was clear and we made good time, but the unending drabness depressed us. Even though the day was lovely, we felt as though it were raining.

We spent the night in Brussels, and we were somewhat revived by the brightly lit squares and the crowds of lively people that clustered around the cafés. After dinner we wandered through the streets until we came to a noisy cabaret, where we passed the rest of the evening watching an absurd striptease performed by a woman who began her act dressed as a witch and ended it by writhing on the floor, naked except for the *cache-sexe,* the token covering demanded by law.

In Holland we stayed with Mr. and Mrs. Jan Roijan in a summer house in Noordwijk aan Zee, a small resort town outside Amsterdam. Bob had written ahead, and the Roijans, friends of his family, had replied that they would be glad to put us up for as long as we could stay.

Since the weather turned poor the day we arrived, sending a chill wind off the North Sea and clouding the sun for five days, we didn't swim. During the day, we rode horseback and walked among the remains of the German bunkers that line the beach.

One afternoon we went walking with Mrs. Roijan. After an hour or so, we stopped for a rest. Bob asked Mrs. Roijan what life in Holland had been like during the war, and she told us of the rationing and the horror and the fright that had come with the Occupation.

"Sometimes we forget," she said. "Sometimes we can put it out of our minds. But then, for no reason at all, something will happen that brings it all back to us. Just recently it happened again."

I asked her what happened.

"Look over there," she said, pointing to a house beyond the dunes. "It happened to the woman in that house, no more than a year ago." She pushed her back deeper into the sand, making a hollow against the wind, and told us the story.

The house stood two hundred yards from the beach, in a clump of pines. From the porch, you could see the remains of the German bunkers, the concrete slabs, the hump in the dune where a tunnel led from pillbox to pillbox. There was barbed wire around the bunkers now, to keep the children from crawling about and falling in one of the holes. The tunnel itself went on for miles along the coast, and there were many other tunnels branching off it. A child could easily lose his way.

The weather had been clear that day, and the breeze from the sea gentle and warmer than usual, so the woman had left the door and windows open while she cleaned. She was in her early sixties, but she moved gracefully. She had no arthitis and no rheumatism, which continued year after year to astonish the other people of the town. Most people succumbed to one or the other after only a few years in the cold, damp climate of the Dutch seashore.

Everything was going well. It had taken fifteen years of work, but the war had been all but erased from her mind.

She wished they would remove the bunkers and the wire, but she was actually quite used to them, and they didn't bother her much. Her husband still limped from the shrapnel the German hand grenade had planted in his leg, but he was better off than many, and he got around perfectly well.

It was the house that had taken all the time. They had lived in the house since they were married, in 1920. They had spent twenty years taking care of it, filling it with themselves, and by 1940 it was as much a part of them as they were of each other. Then the Germans came, and for four years they were away from their house. They lived in small apartments in Amsterdam while the German officers lived in their house. It was a good location, partly hidden from the sea by the trees, yet near enough to make an efficient command post for the bunkers.

When the Germans were driven out, the couple returned home. They had not known what to expect on returning, but certainly not what they found. All the old furniture except two easy chairs had been burned for firewood and replaced by steel barracks furniture. The wallpaper had peeled away, and the walls were scarred and chipped. The paintings of the family were piled in the cellar, some ripped, others only dirty, and had been replaced by pinups of naked and semi-naked girls. The house had apparently never been cleaned, for there were mouse droppings all over the floor and in both remaining easy chairs. The ceilings were black with the soot of the open kerosene lamps the Germans had used when the electricity was cut off.

It was on returning to her home that the woman experienced for the first time a feeling which had all her life seemed nothing more than an abstract word—hate. She had hated the war, and she hated killing and sorrow and pain, but these were feelings that she could not direct anywhere. She could not actively despise war or pain or sorrow. But now she had a hate that was almost tangible. She could feel it in her stomach, and it sometimes made her act in a way that embarrassed her. It was a hatred of all that was German, and though she knew it was unfair, she couldn't help herself. It was not hatred of cruelty or force or strength, for those things she could understand. Like all true hates, hers was something that she could not fully understand—it was of the senseless, animal destruction that the soldiers had wrought on her home. She had believed that man was basically intelligent and good, and the soldiers had shown her to be wrong. She hated the fact that they had punctured her image of man.

But after fifteen years her hate had mellowed and lost its control of her. She had met Germans during those years, tourists mostly, and she had forced herself to accept them. The damage done to her house had been repaired, and once again the house was part of herself. She had allowed herself to forget.

And so she was unprepared for the visitors who came to the house on that mild summer day. She was dusting the paintings, her back to the door, when she felt that someone was in the house. She turned slowly, for she was not alarmed. It was the beginning of the tourist season, and people often stopped by the house to ask their way.

A couple stood on the porch. The man was tall and heavyset. He had close-cropped blond hair that framed a wide, flat, dull face. The woman was tall also, with the body of a peasant girl—big, thick limbs and a solid trunk. She stood with her feet apart. They wore knapsacks with the orange and yellow and black pennants of West Germany hanging off the cover flaps.

"Good day," said the old woman. "Can I help you?"

"*Ja,*" said the man. He stepped through the door into the room. "My wife and I," he said, making a full-arm sweep as a gesture toward his wife, "we are passing through. I would like to show her your house."

"My house?" said the woman. "Why the house? There are many better houses in Noordwijk, many bigger houses. Just down the road there is—"

"No," said the man. "Your house."

"May I ask why?"

"I was here in this house three years during the war. I would like my wife to see where I lived. It is different now from when I was here, but it is the same house."

"No."

The man was puzzled. "What?"

"No," said the woman. Her voice was low, controlled only by great effort. "It is not the same house. It will never be the same house. You will leave."

"But—but it *is* the same house. I know it is the same house."

"It is not! It is not the same house!" The woman's voice was trembling. "Get out!" she screamed. "Get out! This is not the same house!" She ran at the man and began beating him on the chest with her fists.

The man put up his arms to protect himself, and backed through the door. The woman slammed the door just as he stumbled against his wife on the porch.

"Mein Gott!" said the wife. "Why did she do that?"

"I don't know," said the man. "Old fool. The war is over.

Doesn't she know that?" He walked to the door and knocked once, hard. "Hey, lady!" he shouted. "The war is over! You know that, don't you? The war is over!"

There was no answer. After a moment, the man and his wife stepped down off the porch and onto the road.

Inside, the woman leaned against the door. She was sweating, and her hands were shaking.

"It is not over," she said quietly. "I thought so, too. I hoped so. But it is not. It can never be over."

3

W HEN an American college student thinks of Scandinavia, he is seldom concerned with scenery, and almost never concerned with economic theories or political ideas. Technically, his concern is with cultural mores; actually, it is with sex. Over the years, our college students have heard innumerable stories of conquests, easy virtue, free love, and nudist beaches from friends who have spent time abroad. (We choose to remember only our successes, so in time the many failures fade from memory. Or if they do fester like open sores, we never recount them.)

Who has not heard tales of Swedish beauties who sleep with you because they think it's *fun?* Who doesn't have at least one friend who has known a Danish girl who *didn't* demand vows of everlasting love before she would share her

bed? Who, after an unsuccessful date, has not come back to
his room, flopped disgustedly on the couch, and said, "God,
I wish I were in Sweden!"?

Bob had been to Denmark the previous summer with some
friends, and they had returned with wonderful stories of
bacchanalian soirées, some admittedly embellished for effect, some boy-scout's-honor true. He still had a number
of addresses, and as we waited overnight in the car for the
ship from Germany to Gedser, Denmark, we pored over the
names in his little book and he pointed out the virtues and
shortcomings of each lass.

As soon as we were settled in our hotel in Copenhagen,
Bob rang up a girl he had spent considerable time with the
summer before. She was engaged. The second girl he called
was busy all that week, but she would love to see him any
time after the first of the month. Finally, on the fifth try,
he arranged for two dates for that evening.

We picked up the girls at seven. Bob's young lady was
short, dark-haired, with large, exquisite eyes and a full
mouth. She had a body that seemed to have been com-
pounded from all the dreams of every American male—
ample chest (but not *too* ample), narrow waist, shapely legs
and slender ankles. My date was a tall blonde named Inge,
who was studying chemical engineering at the university.
She had fine, sharp features and light blue-gray eyes.

We ate dinner at Oskar Davidson's, the restaurant that has
a sandwich menu four feet long and boasts more than a hundred and thirty different sandwiches. After dinner, we
walked through the Tivoli and listened to the bands and
rode one of the small roller coasters in the amusement park.
When the roller coaster sped through a tunnel and then
swooped down a steep grade, Inge gave a little shriek and

grasped my arm. She did not let it go even when the car
coasted to a stop. I smiled at her, and she looked back at
me with those soft blue eyes and parted her lips in a happy
grin. The tellers of tales had not been lying, I thought, and
I looked forward to later in the evening.

We danced for a while at Nimb, the mammoth dance hall
in the Tivoli, and had some drinks—not too many, though,
since Shakespeare's desire-performance comparison repeated
itself over and over in my mind.

The situation was perfect. The girls lived within a block
of one another, so taking them home, we both used the car.
When Inge and I got to her door, there was no embarrassed
moment, no hemming and hawing, no mere "Thank you
for a lovely evening." She said instead, "Would you come in
for a drink?"

I said I thought I could spare the time.

"Most nights we would have to be very quiet," she said.
"But this weekend my parents are away."

Visions of sugarplums danced in my head. I asked if I
could put some music on the phonograph, and Inge said,
"Of course. But put something soft on. It is too late for
loud music."

I picked a record that looked like quiet, rhythmic mood
music, and put it on. It turned out to be wild jungle yells
and bongo drums, backed up by bird noises and monkey calls.
I fairly tore it off the spindle and put on instead a record by
a man who Inge said was like Jackie Gleason. She translated
the title into English. Roughly, it was "Music To Dream
By."

Inge handed me a Scotch, and we sat on the couch. I undid my tie, and she took off her shoes and curled her feet
underneath her.

"Do you like it here in Denmark?" she asked.

"More every minute," I said, and smiled suggestively at her. I leaned over so that my shoulder just touched her knee.

"I should like to go to America."

"Mmmmmmm?" I said, leaning over a little farther, and tugged at my tie, which had bound itself tightly around my neck.

"Yes," she said. "Oh, does your neck hurt? Here, I will rub it." She put her hand on my neck and began to knead it slowly, sensually, in time with the music.

Here we go, I thought. I turned to the right and put my left hand up to pull her head down to mine.

"Do you know," said Inge, stopping my hand in midair, "that America does not have the position in Europe that it once had?"

"Huh?" I said, and I dropped my hand.

"It is true. I mean, you will have to admit that your standing is not what it was in the 1940's."

"Yeah," I said. "It's a shame." I reached up again for her head.

"It's not that you're not respected," she said, and once more I dropped my hand. "You certainly do have respect. How could anyone help but respect your power? But America is no longer revered. That's it. The reverence that everyone had for America after the war is gone. You are respected, but not revered." She kneaded my neck until it hurt. "Feel better?" she said.

"Swell."

"Good. That always works." She stopped, and reached to the coffee table for a cigarette. "Does your back hurt, too?"

"No," I said. "Why?"

"You're leaning over so far. I thought perhaps you were uncomfortable."

"No. That wasn't what it was." I sat up.

"You have a good President, too," she said. "So that isn't the problem. Mr. Kennedy is liked in Europe."

"I'm glad for him," I said. "It's too bad other people can't be as successful."

"It isn't the people, really. I'm not sure what it is. I guess we feel some sort of resentment about the state of the world."

"I see," I said. "And had we but world enough, and time, I'd love to talk it over with you. But for the moment, can't we forget it?"

"That would be selfish," she said. "Yes, I think it is resentment. I think our people feel that you got us into this mess, and it's up to you to get us out of it. We resent having been dragged into it, and we resent not having been dragged out of it."

"I don't see what I can do about it right now," I said.

"No. But I hope you don't mind my saying those things. I hope you don't resent *me* now."

"Perish the thought," I said.

"Good. I'm glad. Now you must finish your drink. I have to be up early in the morning."

I finished my drink, tightened my tie, and stood up.

"Thank you for the evening," said Inge.

"Not at all," I said. "I'm glad you could come."

"I hope I will see you again before you leave Denmark. I enjoy this kind of conversation, and we see few foreigners to discuss things like this with."

Two minutes later, I was standing on the sidewalk. I walked to the car, wondering whether to drive back to the hotel, spend the night, and come back for Bob in the morning, or to wait in the car. I sat in the car and had a cigarette. It was twenty minutes to two.

At quarter to two the door to Bob's date's house opened, and I saw Bob and the girl standing in the doorway. They talked for a moment, then Bob bent down and kissed the girl on the cheek. She turned and went into the house, and Bob walked toward the car. His hands were jammed into his pockets, and he walked slowly.

"Thank God," he said, when he saw me in the car. "I thought I'd have to wait all night. I was thinking of going back to the hotel."

"So was I. No wonder Hamlet was a melancholy Dane."

4

On July 30 we started our run for the sun, and we drove all day. We spent one night in Germany with some friends of Bob's, the next night in a motel outside Frankfurt, the next in Geneva, and at five o'clock on the afternoon of August 2 we arrived in Cap d'Antibes, Alpes Maritimes (Côte d'Azur), France.

Up to then, we had had no trouble finding rooms. We had spent about half the nights in hotels, the other half staying with various friends or friends of friends. On the Riviera we were stuck. From Grasse, a town above Cannes, I had called some friends of my parents, and they had asked us for dinner the following night, but not, as we had presumptuously assumed they would, to stay with them. There were no rooms free in Juan-les-Pins, a town down the coast

from Cap d'Antibes, or in Cap d'Antibes or even in Antibes
itself. Every Frenchman from every big city in France was
on holiday, and in places like St. Tropez they were sleeping
five or six in a room. We asked waiters, wine stewards,
flower girls, drunks, everyone we saw, where we could get a
room. Most of them just laughed, but some were kind
enough to say, "Impossible, monsieur." Finally, at eleven-
thirty, we persuaded the *patronne* of a small hotel on the
outskirts of Antibes to give us a cellar room for one night,
and in exchange for wads of money we received two cots
and a room the size of a steerage class cabin on a toy boat.
Bob went immediately to bed, and I filled out a traveler's
check and fled to the casino in Antibes.

I have an infallible system for roulette. You divide the
wheel into five sections, like a pie, and put one chip on a
number in the center of each section. This reduces the odds
from 36–1 to around 7–1, and costs you only five times as
much as if you just threw a chip on the number correspond-
ing to the age of Best of Show in last year's Westminster Dog
Show. It's quicker, too. Within an hour I lost my twenty
dollars and went back to our cellar and went to bed. I had
scarcely closed my eyes when there was a rap on the door.
We were told, politely but firmly, that we would have to be
out of our rooms before two. We packed the car and went
to the beach.

In August, the Riviera is hardly the paradise it's cracked
up to be. In addition to the whole French nation, a substan-
tial portion of Germany packs its Volkswagens and scurries
to the Côte d'Azur for camping. Camping—or what the
French pronounce as cam-*peeng*—is an almost entirely German institution. Thousands of Germans jam themselves into
tiny lots, where they unfold their tents and unpack skimpy

bathing suits from their knapsacks. The camps are usually right on the beach, clustered around snack bars. So the whole community is self-contained, and the Germans seldom venture out into the gaudy world of casinos and nightclubs.

The English are there, too. It seems that every English secretary who has saved her shillings during the winter hops down to the Riviera for two weeks in August. They have the reputation of being the loosest girls on the Côte. It's something about not daring to let themselves go all out where people they know can notice and comment, but giving full vent to any and all desires when they're in a foreign country.

Finally, there are the Americans, who, like the French, fall into two categories—the rich vacationers, who fly to the Riviera and fly straight home, and the tourists, en route perhaps from Paris to Florence, who mill around the streets in bikinis and dungarees. In the latter category, the only visible difference between the French and the Americans is that the French are trying to look *nouvelle vague* and the Americans are trying to look French.

Life is not hectic. One rises late (unless he lives in that cellar) and goes immediately to the beach, to lie in the sun and squirm on the rocks. Those who can afford it water-ski or skin-dive. The others just swim in the clear water and get second-degree burns on parts of their bodies that are never otherwise exposed—either to human eyes or to the sun. When the sun goes down, the men walk the streets in sandals and dungarees and form-fitting T shirts, the women in toreador pants and bare-midriff blouses. They eat at Pam-Pam, and they dance outside Whisky à Gogo if they can't afford the two or three dollars admission. They sit in the cafés and drink beer or Perrier and talk about what they did that day or have planned for the next. The very wealthy

give parties and serve whisky, and the sounds of babbling
voices and raucous music spill down the rocks from the great
villas to the people necking on the beach.

That night we drove to dinner, prepared to sleep either in
the car or on the beach until we could get a room. Neither
of us realized that dinner would last for two weeks.

Mr. and Mrs. Oliver Rea had taken a villa in Cap
d'Antibes for the summer. It was called "Le Ponant," and
it sat on a hillside a few hundred yards from the shore. Mr.
Rea, a theatrical producer who has recently opened a theater
in Minneapolis, had settled his wife and three children in
the villa for the summer and was commuting between
Antibes and New York and Minneapolis, spending two or
three weeks in each place. After a delicious dinner, we
explained our plight to the Reas and asked if they had any
suggestions. They named two or three places, which we tried
and found either full or way up in the mountains, too far
away from Antibes to be convenient. When all possibilities
had been exhausted, the Reas, out of pity, desperation,
incredibly kind hearts, and a feeling that since Mr. Rea
would be away for a while and there would be no other
guests it might not be a bad idea to have two sizable hulks
around a house full of women and children, offered to put
us up themselves. We demurred for perhaps twenty seconds,
then sublimated both conscience and politeness and accepted
eagerly. Our only attempt at good manners was to insist
that the Reas tell us when they wanted us to leave, to which
they just as eagerly agreed.

The life was blissful. The Reas had a cabana at Eden
Roc, the swimming club on the Cap that offers some of the
only good swimming on the Riviera and a choice of both
pool or sea, and they very nicely said we could use it as we

wished. So during the day we frolicked about Eden Roc, jumping off the thirty-foot cliffs, swinging on ropes, meeting young ladies, and hunting for octopus among the rocks. Lunch was a Coca-Cola or a beer. Our days were shamefully devoid of responsibilities and useful endeavor, and we loved it.

Our nights were active. The Reas had a number of friends in and around Antibes, and there were always parties, dinners, or excursions up and down the coast to keep us occupied. Sometimes we went to the casinos, where I practiced my infallible system, or to Vence to watch the fireworks, or to Cannes to see some friends.

On the 16th of August, Mr. Rea returned and told us that since they were planning to have guests the following weekend, we would have to vacate our rooms before Saturday, as per the agreement we made at the start. Although we were enjoying ourselves, we were not unhappy at the prospect of moving on. We had had two weeks of complete lassitude, devoid of any responsibility, and as pleasant as it had been, we felt we should see something more during the summer than the Côte d'Azur.

So on Saturday we started for Spain, after presenting the Reas with a case of wine, two cap pistols, and a toy car.

That night I had to send a cable home. My camera had been stolen from the car while we were packing to leave the Reas, and I wanted to notify the insurance company of the loss. Apparently, the thief was one of the men repairing the road to Eden Roc. The workers take a long lunch hour, and to avoid the hot August sun they often crawl in among the bushes, where they can eat their bread and drink their wine and nap for half an hour. One of these workers must have been watching us pack, for the camera disappeared in a space of two minutes while Bob and I were in the house getting our suitcases.

We had stopped at a small hotel in Béziers, a town at the foot of the Pyrenees a few miles from the Spanish border. The people of Bézier speak neither French nor Spanish, but Basque, the language of the Costa Brava, which is a combination of French, Spanish, Italian, and a mysterious eastern language no one can identify. When I found myself unable to communicate with the concierge in the hotel, I wrote out the cable in French, English, and my own Spanish, which bears little or no resemblance to any Spanish the world has ever known. I heard later that the message, as it arrived in New York, read, "Appareil stolen dos Aout, Costa Azul. Please contactame sueno de American Express, Madrid, Espagne."

Only tourists and masochists go to Madrid in the summer. Sitting on a plateau in the barren, parched Spanish countryside, the city seems to be reaching for the sun, and the sun is all too willing to smother it. From one to four in the afternoon, the streets are deserted. People lie in doorways out of the sun or huddle close to the moist tile walls of the restaurants and gulp sangría, the fruit and wine drink that is perfectly harmless—for the first pint or two, after which the ceiling begins to spin and two large hands pull downward on your eyelids.

It is a city of smells. We ate in the *tascas*, which are tiny, cheap luncheon joints cut out of the walls of the low buildings. From early morning until late evening, the odors of the tascas are everywhere. Side streets are full of the smell of fried squid, salami, peppers, fish, cheese, and beer. They do not quite blend, like normal smells, because they are too strong. Each one is so highly, and so individually, spiced that it stands out and prickles your nose, demanding to be noticed.

We slept late, lying naked on sweat-soaked sheets. At noon, we hurried to the bar and had breakfast, a glass of orange juice, and read the papers. We ran across the street and checked our mail, then fled to the nearest tasca for lunch. After lunch, if we had no plans to go sightseeing, we went to the Prado and sat in one of the badly lit rooms, basking in the dark coolness and glancing idly at the Bosches and Goyas. We slept or read from five to seven, when we dressed and went to the bar. We drank, alone or with friends, until nine-thirty or ten, when most restaurants began to get crowded. We ate until twelve or one, then walked around the city or went to one of the many nightclubs.

One afternoon, as we were coming out of the Prado, we saw two middle-aged women coming in. They had cameras and dark glasses and foam-rubber-soled shoes. One of them carried a copy of *Europe On Five Dollars A Day*. They bought tickets and went to the stand where postcards and guidebooks were sold. One of them asked for a guidebook.

"Which one you like?" asked the man behind the counter.

"The one with the names of all the pictures and the order they're in," said one of the women.

The man gave her a book.

"How much?"

"Sixty pesetas," said the man.

The woman reached in her pocketbook and brought out a fistful of money. "Here," she said, holding out her hand. "Pick it out of there."

The man took sixty pesetas, and the woman dumped the rest of the money into her pocketbook. "Didn't take any more than sixty, did you?"

"No, madam."

"Good. Can't be too careful," she said to her friend.

The other woman wandered away from the counter and studied the racks of postcards.

"Carol!" shouted the first woman. "Come *on!* We can't waste any time if we're going to see this whole place."

"Yes, Edna. What time does the tour leave?"

"Four o'clock sharp. That leaves us forty-five minutes to do the Prado."

"Where are we going this afternoon, Edna?"

"Out of town somewhere. Toledo, I think."

"What's there?"

"How do I know? Steel or something. At least, that's what the book says. Now come on. If we get through early, you can come back to the postcards."

"Do we *have* to, Edna?"

"Of course we have to. What would the folks back home say if they knew we'd been in Madrid without seeing the Prado? It's like the Eiffel Tower."

"Oh, all right."

Edna turned to the man behind the counter. "Hey, you," she said. "Are you sure this book has all the pictures?"

"Yes, madam."

"Room by room? In order?"

"Yes, madam."

"Good. Where do we start?"

"There, madam," said the man, pointing to the left.

"Thanks. Here," said Edna, and she handed the book to her friend. "Have you got your pencil?"

"Yes, Edna."

"Good. Now let's go. I'll look and you check."

The Sunday before we left Spain, we went to a bullfight. There were six fights, all with *novilleros*, young matadors who had either never fought in a big arena before or never proved themselves to be worthy of the best bulls. Since these were to be our only fights, we splurged and got decent tickets, halfway up the stands on the sunny side of the arena. The best seats were across the way, in the shade, but ours were more than adequate. We went with a friend, Jim Dooley, who had spent the summer studying Spanish in Madrid, and he brought two wineskins full of a mixture of gin and sangría.

Most of the pageant at a bullfight happens before the actual combat. The whole company, banderilleros, picadors, horses, and matadors, marches around the arena as the trumpets play the exciting staccato music of the ring. Announcements are made over the loudspeakers, and the bulls are brought out to be taunted by all the matadors, who make showy, safe passes. Finally, the bulls are herded out and the ring quiets down. The first bull returns through the small door. The fun is over, and the game is being played in earnest.

As soon as the first bull was in the ring, he stopped, confused and blinded by the sudden light and space and noise. He shook his head from side to side and made quick, uncertain lunges at an invisible enemy. The picador, his long spear, the *pic*, held high, began to move his horse across the ring toward the bull. The bull spied the horse, charged a few yards toward him, then stopped. The picador moved closer.

When the picador was within ten yards of the bull, the bull lowered his head, pawed the ground once, and charged. The picador lowered his spear. The bull took the spear in the thick muscle of his neck, and immediately blood began to spread over his black coat, but he did not stop. He drove his horns into the padding on the horse's side and moved his head up and down, trying to lift the padding and get to the flesh beneath. The horse, unable to see because of the blinders, gave with the weight of the bull and stumbled sideways. The picador pulled out his spear and moved the horse a few feet away. The bull stood still, panting. Blood flowed over his shoulders and dripped to the sand.

On the second charge, the picador lowered his spear early and caught the bull before he could get to the horse. He held the bull away for a moment, then removed the spear and guided the horse to safety. The bull charged again, the picador lowered his spear, and hit the bull a glancing blow on the shoulder. The spear skidded out of his hand. The bull hit the horse on the underside of the padding and lifted his two left feet off the ground. The bull pulled back, then hit again. The horse fell over, and the man scrambled to his feet and ran to the side of the ring. The audience booed. Two men ran into the ring and diverted the bull from the horse, who rolled back onto his feet and trotted away.

The first banderillero approached the bull in the center of the ring. He came up from the side, not from the front, and sank one *banderilla*, the short, razor-sharp spear, into the weakened neck, the other into the back. He made a sweeping gesture of acknowledgment of an applause that did not exist, and ran off. The second banderillero dropped both banderillas, but not before he had sliced a large gash in the bull's forehead. The third drove both into the neck, and they hung loosely from the flesh, bouncing gaily as the bull ran around the ring.

The bull stood in the shade. His head hung lower now, for his neck was very weak. Blood ran into one eye from the gash on his forehead, and over his back and shoulders from the other cuts. There were circular trails of blood in the sand where he had tried to catch the banderilleros on their quick passes.

The trumpets sounded, and the matador entered the ring. He was a young man, slim and erect, and he wore a pea-green costume covered with sequins. The crowd cheered, but the cheer was one of courtesy rather than enthusiasm, for this was a boy as yet untried, and he had to prove himself to them that afternoon. Later, they might be his fans, as they were of Dominguín and Ordóñez and Ostos. Now they were his judges.

The boy walked around the edge of the ring toward the bull, keeping out of his way until he could come up behind him and drive him into the sunlight, where the bull had no advantage. When they were close to the center of the ring, the bull charged. The boy moved back a step and had to lean over to get the cape in front of the bull. The crowd booed. The bull would not charge again. He stood looking at the boy. The bull's breathing was deep, and blood ran off his face. The boy moved closer, and the bull took three steps forward and twisted his head dully. The boy moved a few feet away and stood in a cocky, defiant pose. He stamped his foot on the sand, trying to goad the bull into charging him. The bull looked at him, then lowered his head and trotted toward him. The boy stood his ground, but again bent his body away from the horns. Again the crowd booed.

"Mátalo!" yelled the crowd. "Kill him!"

On his next approach, the bull, blinded by his own blood, missed the cape and bumped against the boy, knocking him down.

"Mátalo!"

The boy walked to the side of the ring and exchanged his

large cape for a smaller one, the one with the killing sword. He walked back to the bull, who stood, head bowed, in the center of the ring. The boy aimed carefully, for a clean kill was the only thing that could give him even partial credit for the fight. The bull trotted toward him, and the boy bent over the horns and drove the sword in. He missed the space between the shoulders that leads to the heart, and the sword stuck in a muscle, swaying back and forth like a metronome. The bull turned his head and looked at the sword with a sort of blasé curiosity. The boy walked to the side of the ring and got another sword.

A woman threw an apple. A man threw a chicken leg. Suddenly everyone was throwing things—papers, garbage, seat cushions.

The boy lunged again. The sword hit a bone and would not go in. The boy was furious. He chased the bull from the rear, ran around him, and stopped him. He jammed the sword in with both hands. The bull made a lazy pass at him with his head, but missed.

The sword had not struck the heart, but the bull was dying anyway, from loss of blood. He sank to his knees. Two men came from the side of the ring and stood with the boy. When, after a moment, the bull still lived, one of the men bent over and with a quick flick of a small knife, slit the bull's throat. The bull fell over onto his side, breathed for a few seconds more, and was dead.

The boy left the ring at the nearest exit. His head was bowed, and his shoulders were shaking.

The second fight lasted longer, but the result was the same: the men had to come from the sidelines to slit the bull's throat.

The third bull was what Dooley called a "hooker." When he charges, a hooker doesn't make a straight pass, but hooks his head to the left or right. A matador has to be doubly wary of a hooker, because while he can gauge how a normal bull is going to carry his horns, he is never sure a hooker won't drive a horn into his groin with a sudden twist of his head.

The bull was beautiful, a heavy, fast, black hulk that didn't stop when it entered the ring but ran straight for the horse and knocked him up against the wall. He didn't seem to feel the pic in his neck, and kept trying to force his way into the horse's ribcage.

The picadors and banderilleros worked hard to make this bull safe. They picked him seven times, until his head hung low and he swung it wearily from side to side. All six banderillas stuck like needles in his neck. The horses ran him around the ring to tire him.

"They don't like the odds," said Dooley. "They're too even."

The crowd began to boo, but just then the matador came into the ring, and they stopped. As soon as the bull spotted the matador, he charged. The matador planted his feet and held out the cape. As the bull passed, he twisted his head sharply to the left, narrowly missing the matador's side. The crowd cheered. The bull skidded to a stop in front of the wall. He turned and charged again. The matador took the pass on the bull's right side, avoiding the hook. This time the cheer was more polite than enthusiastic.

"The passes are all show," said Dooley. "If that bull didn't hook, they'd be throwing garbage at the kid. He doesn't stand close enough. If he avoids the hook side again, you'll hear some catcalls."

The matador took the bull on his right side again, and the people booed. Then he stopped for a moment, looking at the bull. He held the cape in his right hand, and he turned his right side toward the bull, holding the arm with the cape across his body so the cape was on his left side.

"He's going to take him on the left," said Dooley.

The bull charged. He hooked early, and though the matador spun to get out of the way, a horn caught him in his right buttock, and he fell down. Blood began to seep through a tear in his blue pants.

"Well, damn well about time, too," said Bob.

"Serves the bastard right," I said.

Two men with capes ran into the ring and coaxed the bull away from the matador.

On the next pass, the matador faltered and backed away. The bull turned and started for the cape, which was held on the safe side, then swerved and hit the matador full in the stomach with his head. Somehow, the horns passed to either side of the slim body, and the matador was thrown in the air.

"Thataboy!" yelled Bob.

"Give him a stomp for good measure!" I shouted.

The matador was stunned, but not hurt. He hurried to his feet, picked up his cape, and approached the bull. He made two clean passes, but both on the safe side and both ordinary, unimaginative passes. The crowd booed.

The boy tried once again to take the bull on the hook side. This time, the horn hit his thigh and tore a hole in his pants, but did not draw blood. By now, the blood from the wound in his buttock was running down his leg.

"Mátalo!" yelled the crowd.

"*Mátalo*, hell!" answered Bob. "Let the bull go! They let the gladiators go when they fought well, didn't they? Hey, Dooley, how do you scream 'let him go' in Spanish?"

"I'm not sure," said Dooley. "Try '*déjalo!*'"

"Déjalo!" shouted Bob.

The matador went to the side of the ring to get the killing sword. The wound in his buttock had stiffened his leg, and he limped. When he had the sword, he came back to the center of the ring and faced the bull. The bull pawed the sand and charged. The matador jumped out of the way, and the crowd booed. The bull turned and stood looking at the matador. The boy moved slowly forward, placing each foot carefully. When he was only a few feet from the bull's horns, he stopped. He moved one step to his left.

"He's not going to go straight in," said Bob. "He's moving away from the hook and is going in over the side."

I yelled, "Chicken!"

The boy moved two steps closer, and as the bull lowered his head, he leapt in over the right horn and sunk the sword into the neck. It was no kill. The sword had gone in only a few inches. The boy reached up from behind the bull and pulled it out. The crowd hooted. The woman next to me threw a beer bottle into the ring.

The second thrust was deep, but not a clean kill. The bull wrenched his head to the left and knocked the boy spinning, then fell to his knees. He knelt there, shaking his head and drooling.

"He's blind now," said Dooley. "That's why he's moving his head like that, sort of desperate defense."

The bull would not die. The boy reached over the horns and pulled the sword out and jammed it in again. And again. The bull called out in a low groan. The boy was shaking. His fists were clenched, and Dooley could see through his binoculars that he was crying. He began to beat the bull on the neck with the sword, as if trying to decapitate it.

Four men ran into the ring. They positioned themselves around the bull and waved their capes over his body. The bull struggled to his feet and heaved his body around in circles, tossing his head. I asked Dooley what that was for.

"It circulates the blood," he said. "If his heart was even scratched, it'll kill him quickly. If not, then they do it till he bleeds to death. It speeds things up."

The boy had stopped beating the bull, and stood to one side, tears running down his face. Finally, one of the men hit the bull with his hip and knocked him over. He bent down and slit the bull's throat.

We left after the third fight. On the way back into the city, Bob was silent. Then, as we were parking the car, he said simply, "Jesus."

"I know," I said. "Pretty ghastly."

"It's not that," said Bob. "What bothers me is me. I just this minute realized what I was cheering for this afternoon. I was cheering for a man to get killed. Or maimed. And I'd probably go again, too, just hoping some matador will get gored. Jesus."

When we got to the hotel, we went straight to the bar, where we stayed until one in the morning.

5

WE DROVE north along the west coast of France, through Biarritz and the Loire country and Chartres. Bob had to be in Paris by the first of September to take entrance exams for a graduate school of the Sorbonne, so we couldn't dawdle on the way back. But we didn't have to drive straight through, either, so we took two days off and lay on the beach at Biarritz. It was there that Bob got a letter from his father telling him to get off the beaches. "Every word from you in the past month has come from the seashore," read the letter. "Don't you think it might be nice if you moved inland for a while, just to see what the country is like?" We spent an evening experimenting with new infallible systems at the Biarritz casino, and moved on.

As soon as we got to Paris, we started looking for an

apartment. We again took a room in the Hôtel St. Paul,
which suited us well financially, but still we had only one
room. We had been staying in hotels for over two months,
and we wanted more space.

The search lasted less than a week. Through friends of
friends of friends, we met a woman whose mother had recently died and left her with a furnished apartment on the
Rue de Saint Simon, a small street off the Boulevard St.
Germain, near the Rue du Bac. She asked us to look at the
apartment. What we had wanted was a small apartment,
preferably with two bedrooms. What we found was a small
palace. Two bedrooms, indeed. And two living rooms, a
large foyer, a dining room with a table big enough for ten,
and a huge kitchen. And every room, except the kitchen
and the smaller of the two living rooms, furnished Louis
XVI. The price, we were told, was a terribly reasonable $260
per month. How, wondered the landlady, could we turn
down such a bargain?

"Much too much," I said.

"You're right," said Bob. "It's nice, though."

"Sure, it's nice. But so is Versailles."

"I guess you're right."

"There is one thing," I said. "We'd probably never get
a chance like this again, to live in a place like this for that
money."

"Mmm."

"I mean, I just thought I'd bring it up while we were
considering all sides of the situation."

"And we *have* been looking around," said Bob. "No one
can accuse us of jumping in blind."

"We certainly have. And we haven't found anything even
halfway decent."

"No. Anyway, nothing like this."

"And that St. Paul *is* getting cramped."

"Besides," said Bob, "what reason have we to believe that we'll ever find anything better than this?"

"None whatsoever. That's a good point. We might even get thrown out of the St. Paul, and then where would we be? With no place to go, that's where."

Bob looked pensive. "We can't," he said. "It's just too expensive."

"I know," I said. "Let's take it."

"You're on."

Life at 15 Rue de Saint Simon was not a great deal more productive than life at the St. Paul, but it was infinitely more pleasant. I entered the Alliance Française, the language school where foreigners learn French. My French was all right, but I felt that it was not beyond improvement. Bob attended classes at the Sorbonne. We read the papers (American for news, French for practice), went to a few museums, and walked around what is to me the most beautiful city in the world.

At night, if we didn't go to a theater or a movie, we dined late and long, usually at a restaurant on St. Germain called Il Teatro. In August, Il Teatro had been bombed. A *plastique* had been set off by the front door, and it had blown out the door, the plate glass window, and six light fixtures in the front of the restaurant. The owners' first thought was that the bombing was the work of Algerian terrorists, though Il Teatro had taken no stand on political issues and was harboring no extremist from either side. Within ten days, the culprit was caught, after he had blown out the windows and doors of four more establishments in the neighborhood. He was a manufacturer of plate glass

windows, and he had been periodically bombing the stores
and restaurants in his neighborhood that had big plate glass
windows. He explained to the police that business was bad,
and he had only been trying to drum up some trade.

At 15 Rue de Saint Simon we were mother-henned by our
concierge, a woman of sixty-three named Mme. Cuillet.
Mme. Cuillet lived with her husband on the ground floor,
and our apartment was directly above hers. Thus she knew
what time we came in, how many people we had for parties,
how late women guests were staying compared to men guests,
and, since we had to ask her advice about cooking, what we
had for every meal. She had only one complaint, and she
used to voice it regularly. The first time she brought it up,
she almost gave me a coronary. I had slept late, and I answered the door in my shorts.

She stood in the doorway, her hands on her hips, peering
over her rimless glasses. "Bonjour, Monsieur Peters," she
said. She had long since given up trying to pronounce
Benchley.

"Bonjour, madame," I said, stifling a yawn.

"You had two young ladies here last night. Very late."

Oh, good God, I thought, she's going to start spying for
the landlady. I said nothing, but looked at her with a stupid
grin.

"You will do me a great favor," she said, "if you will have
your young ladies remove their shoes late at night."

"Madame?"

"If you please. It keeps my husband and me from sleeping,
to hear the clic-clac of the heels on the wood floor above
our heads."

"I am very sorry, madame. It won't happen again."

"Good," she said. "You will excuse me for bothering you."

She turned to go. "One more thing, if you will permit. Please do not have your young ladies slam the refrigerator door at two o'clock in the morning."

"Yes, madame. Once again, I apologize."

"It is nothing. How was your food?"

"Excellent, thanks to you."

"Good. Au revoir, Monsieur Peters."

"Au revoir, Madame Cuillet."

Two days later, Mme. Cuillet told us that the landlady had been inquiring about our conduct. Mme. Cuillet had told her that she knew nothing about our conduct, but she did say that we were very quiet and never disturbed her.

One evening at a party, I was standing by the bar when I was approached by a young man of approximately my own age.

"You're American," he said.

"Yes."

"Is this the first party you've been to in Paris?" He was French, but he spoke English with a crisp British accent. I would have been unsure of his nationality had he not half swallowed the *r* in 'Paris.'

"No. Why do you ask?"

"Curiosity, really. Very few Americans are invited to French parties."

"Should I feel honored?"

"In a way. It means the host doesn't think of you as a typical American."

"And what do you and the host consider a 'typical' American?" I asked.

"You know, the hail-fellow-well-met type. Horrid clothes, lots of noise, and no taste in anything or for anything except

money. The kind that thinks culture means anything that
appears on the telly."

"You really think that's the average American?"

"I suppose not, but it's the kind we see most of over here.
How else can we judge?"

"Do you consider yourself an average Frenchman?"

"Well, I . . ." he stopped. "No, not really."

"How are you above average?"

"Money and education."

"And how many average Frenchmen do you know?"

"If you take average to mean middle-class businessman
types, the shopkeepers and small industry people, I know
some."

"Socially?"

"Not actually socially, no. I mean, I don't go out with
them."

"Suppose you were to give five hundred thousand new
francs, about a hundred thousand dollars, to your 'average'
Frenchman," I said. "What do you think he'd do with it?"

"He certainly wouldn't rush off to a strange country and
buy ghastly clothes and a big car and smoke cigars and try
to buy everything and everyone he met, I can tell you that."

"How do you know he wouldn't?"

"I just know, that's all. The average Frenchman has better
taste than that. He dresses conservatively, he goes to the
opera, he—"

"He goes to the opera?"

"I think so. A friend of mine said he saw his butcher at
the opera the other night. They read, too. And their table
manners are far superior to almost any American's I've seen."

"Any way," I said, "what *would* your average Frenchman
do with the money?"

"He'd make improvements on his house, maybe decorate it. He might buy a place in the country. He'd send his children to good schools and dress his wife in fine clothes."

"I'll tell you what I think he'd do with it. He'd—" A girl I had been waiting for tapped me on the arm and said that Bob was waiting downstairs with the car, so the conversation ended.

As the weeks went by, we got to know our grocer well. A young man with a wife and two children, he runs one of his father's two grocery stores. Although both stores are mortgaged and he and his father live on salaries, they make between four and six thousand dollars a year, which is much higher than the national average. Still, it does not qualify them for the upper middle class. It seemed to me that he fitted perfectly the description of the "average" Frenchman that the man at the party had given.

Sometimes the grocer, whose name was Maurice, stopped by for a drink after work, and twice or three times a week Bob or I would have coffee with him in a café across the street from his store. When we had known him for over a month and had invited him to two of our parties, he asked us to dinner at his apartment.

To get to Maurice's apartment, we had to walk through the bottle storage room of his father's store, the French equivalent of a Safeway or an A & P, but considerably smaller. The room was lit by a 25-watt bulb, and I barked my shins twice on cases of Coca-Cola and Perrier bottles. We were met at the door by Maurice's wife, Yvonne, a pretty, dark-haired girl with a bawdy laugh that had stopped conversations both times she had come to our house.

"Gooood eeveneeeng," she said.

I said I hadn't known she spoke English.

"I want to learn," she said in French. "You will have to teach me."

Maurice greeted us. He said they had just had the apartment repainted, and he would be happy to show us around. It was a small apartment, two bedrooms, a living room, and a tiny kitchen, furnished in what Bob described as bastard green-stamp baroque. A watercolor of a maroon-haired, hazel-eyed Christ in a twisted gold frame occupied the place of honor on the mantelpiece. The furniture in the living room consisted of one red plastic chair, one green plastic chair, two yellow straightback plastic chairs, and a big plastic table painted to look like wood and adorned with brass knobs on the legs. The tablecloth was a square of red-and-white-checked oilcloth. Three standup lamps with white plastic shades flecked with gold, and two wrought-iron end tables (matching) were placed around the room. In the master bedroom, a hand-colored photograph of Maurice's father hung over the double bed facing a watercolor of a maroon-haired, hazel-eyed Virgin on the opposite wall.

When he had first invited us, Maurice had apologized for the dinner. "It will not be like what you serve," he said. "Meat like that, my God! We never see it. Meat is not a big part of our diet. Too expensive." And as we sat down to eat, he apologized again. "I know you like meat," he said, "but perhaps you will enjoy a salad." The dinner was vegetable soup, shrimp salad, cheese, and a *vin de table*.

Yvonne pointed her fork at me. "You must talk to Maurice," she said. "He wants to buy a car. It is stupid. He has a car."

"I have a car, yes, but it is old."

Bob asked what kind of car he had.

"A DS–19, but an old one," said Maurice. The DS–19 is

the French Cadillac, the car made by Citroën that French
businessmen use for limousines. Some people call it "the
fish" because of its low, sloping front end.

"Why do you want a new one?" I asked. "The DS–19's
look the same from year to year."

"I didn't say a new DS–19. I may get a Jaguar."

"A Jaguar!" shouted Yvonne, and a piece of shrimp flew
out of her mouth. She slammed her fork down on the table.
"And after that perhaps a yacht and an airplane?"

"But have you seen the people who drive the Jaguar? That
is an automobile. It has real chic."

"We need many things before a Jaguar," said Yvonne.
"But if you want to throw your pennies away, you can take
me to the Côte d'Azur." She turned to me. "After dinner
you must tell me about the Côte d'Azur. I have always
dreamed of living in a villa with lots of servants. They have
that there, no?"

"They have that there," I said.

"Oh, if we had the money, there are such magnificent
things we could do!"

"What would you do?" I asked.

"Buy a Jaguar," said Maurice.

"And go to the Côte d'Azur for four months a year," said
Yvonne, "and have new clothes and a fine apartment."

"We would also buy a lot of meat," said Maurice. "Every
night we would have meat."

"You and your meat," sniffed Yvonne. "You have lived all
your life without so much meat. You could live a little
longer."

At a party a few days later I met the captious young man
who had felt so strongly about the hideousness of the Ameri-

can middle class, and I told him about our dinner with
Maurice. He conceded that the "average" Frenchman might
not be all he had made him out to be, but the concession in
no way softened his harangue against Americans. He seemed
obsessed with trying to prove the cultural superiority of the
French.

One group of Americans that he seemed to be almost fanat-
ical about was what he called "the bearded ones," the beat-
niks. "They are all over Paris," he said. "And they stick
out like pustules on the face of the city."

I was in no position to argue with him about these particular members of the American expatriate set, for Bob and
I had almost no contact with them. Our lack of association
with them was not entirely our own choice. We would have
been interested in spending some time with them, to see how
they lived, what they thought, and what they were accom-
plishing. But by our dress, our friends, and our interests,
we would have been classified by them as squarer than
square: "Cube, man."

We did meet one member of this set, however. His name
is Gino, and we had heard about him often, from bartenders,
from our own friends, and from eavesdropping on conversations in cafés. We had seen him shuffling down St. Germain
or bending over a bar in deep conversation with the bartender. If we were going to meet any of the group, we
thought, Gino was the one, the extreme example, the proto-
type of the American beatnik abroad. Even before we finally
did meet him, we knew the following about him:

Gino has two possessions, a beard and a guitar. I had
never seen his guitar, but I hoped it was in better shape than
his beard, which is not a good one. It is long and scraggly,
and it grows wild and untrimmed, like black underbrush
flecked with brown. It catches food. His beard does two

things for his appearance: first, it complements his clothes, which are always drab and usually filthy; second, it hides a hideous set of teeth—brown, crooked, stumpy teeth that can not have been brushed for years.

No one knows where Gino will be at a given time. For more than five years he has been traveling from city to city in Europe, living off his friends, who are, almost to a man, American expatriates something like himself. He never asks for much—five dollars from this one, three dollars from that one, and they're always "loans," with a smile. When asked what he does, Gino replies that he is studying guitar. He has been studying guitar for a long time. How much longer will he be studying guitar? He doesn't know. Most of the time he wanders. He sits in cafés talking to people who claim to be writers or painters. He goes to someone's room, and they sit on the floor and listen to music.

Other than his expatriate comrades, Gino has few friends. He does, however, have a number of acquaintances. He has been around for so long, people know him. Barmaids, waitresses, prostitutes, saloon sitters. He can always cadge a drink or a cigarette. If someone wearies of giving Gino handouts, he scorns that person as someone who doesn't know the rules. "Man, it's like this. When I have something, you get half. When you have something, I get half. It works, man, it works." But Gino never has anything.

I met Gino in a Paris *discothèque*, a bar where one can dance to recorded music. I had stopped in to have a drink on my way home, and I sat alone at a small corner table. Gino was also alone, at the table next to me. The room was dark, and at the tables nearby, people were sitting, eyes closed, listening to a moody Brubeck side. Gino leaned over to me and said, "Hey, man, got an extra cigarette?"

I gave him a cigarette and lit it for him, and he gave me

a perfunctory nod, as though that was all so small a gift deserved. A few tables away, a lone girl rocked back and forth in her chair. She seemed to be in a sort of trance. Her head moved slowly up and down, and her lips were glistening wet. I asked Gino who she was.

"The Nodder," he said. "Look at her go. Man, she's really on it tonight."

"On it?"

"Yeah. Pot. You know, man. A little screwing, a little pot, a little booze, and she'll sit like that all night." He sipped the cheap brandy that he had bummed from the bartender. A man in a blue suit came to the table and tapped Gino on the shoulder. "Hey, man," said Gino. "Grab a chair."

"Can't," said the man. "I have to meet Jimmy at the Maggots. So we'll see you."

"Yeah. I'll be here." The man walked away. "That's Eddie. You know who Jimmy is? Jimmy Baldwin. The writer. Now there's a cool guy. Five thousand skins he just got for an advance on a book he ain't even written. Not bad."

"Is Eddie a writer too?" I said.

"Yeah."

"Is he successful?"

"That depends, man. What do you mean by successful?"

"Commercially."

"Man, who needs it? He's got all the success he needs. Who needs the commercial stuff?"

"Does anyone read him?"

"Why, sure, man. I read his stuff. And Mailer and Baldwin and Jones have read it, too. Man, he's got it."

"Does he have anything to say?"

"You know it, man."

"Well, doesn't he want people to read what he has to say?"

"I told you, man, *we* read it."

"I mean the general public."

"The general public ain't got no more brains than a bug. Man, you can't tell the general public nothing. Your general public don't understand nothing. I could tell the general public a thing or two. I could tell more people than that, too. I could tell that fink in the White House a thing or two."

"Like what?"

"Look, man, that guy's trying to get us all blowed up over here. He's trying, and he's going to do it, too, if somebody don't do something."

"If who doesn't do what?"

"Anybody, man, anybody. What good's them bombs? He's gonna get us all blowed to hell. He *wants* to. He's crazy."

"Why don't *you* do something?"

"I been thinking about it, and I'm gonna. My old man's got a friend of his on the *New York Times*. I'm gonna write and have it printed that I challenged that fink in the White House to a television debate. You know, one of them things like they did at the election. We'll get on television and we'll talk about all them bombs."

"What do you want him to do?"

"The bombs, man. Get rid of all them bombs."

"And the Russians?"

"Ah, screw the Russians."

"Easier said than done."

"Just screw them, them and their bombs. They're no good, man."

"That's too simple, Gino."

"That's what we need, man, a little simpleness around here. All the foreign policy guys don't know nothing. Alls they do is talk, while that fink tries to get us all blowed up."

I was going to say something further when Gino suddenly got up from the table. "Cool it, man. I gotta move," he said.

"Yeah," I said. "I'll be looking in the papers for your debate."

"You do it, man." He turned toward the bar. "*Merci* for the booze, man," he said to the bartender. On his way out, he stopped to bum a cigarette from a man at the door.

What I wondered was, would Gino remember to wear a blue shirt instead of a white one, so he doesn't get a glare from the studio lights?

6

IN LATE September, a Russian exposition opened at the great hall of the Porte de Versailles. It was billed as an exhibit of goods from all aspects of Russian life, from farm to city, from clothes to space capsules.

Bob and I took the subway partway, then walked for a mile or so, enjoying the warm autumn sun. When we were three or four hundred yards away from the Porte de Versailles, I stopped. "Look!" I said, pointing at the hall. A Russian flag, perhaps ten feet by twelve, floated lazily over the building.

"Good God!" he said. "They've landed."

The nearer we got, the more flags we saw, gold hammers and sickles on red backgrounds. I had never seen the Communist standards in such numbers, had never been towered

over by photographs of Lenin and Khrushchev and signs
saying URSS, and for a moment I felt uneasy.

The hall itself was mammoth, and packed with material
and verbal tributes to Russian progress. On the walls were
hung plaster tablets painted to look like marble, which displayed the sculptured figures and sayings of Russia's greats.
Beside a picture of Lenin at the entrance was a tablet which
said, *Paix, Education, Culture, Les Trois Buts du Peuple
Russe,* and under a flattering bust of Khrushchev was the
simple phrase, *Education Pour Tous.* Various anonymous
heroes had contributed such statements as, *Le Progrès So-
viétique Est la Meilleur Preuve des Merveilles de la Vie Com-
muniste,* and *1970—l'URSS le Plus Grand Pouvoir Industriel
du Monde.* Crowded around the walls were booths of optical
devices, radio-spectographs, computers, scale model factories,
full-size automobiles, books, watches, cameras, engines, television sets, tractors, model cranes made by the students of
such-and-such a school in Smolensk, and pictures of full-
bosomed Soviet belles swinging scythes in the bright Ukrain-
ian sunshine. In the center of the floor, a full-scale copy of
Gagarin's capsule twirled sedately next to a model of the
rocket that had sent it up.

On a second level, reached by a spiral staircase that was
apparently suspended from nothing, were models of all the
best Soviet aircraft. Each plane was hung from a thin, almost
invisible wire that led to the ceiling, some twenty feet higher.
Two closed-circuit television sets, one on either side of the
platform, were there to give visitors a running commentary
about the planes, featuring films about the development and
performance of each one.

There were four rooms off the main hall, and they contained a movie theater that would from time to time present

representative Russian films, a room of Russian paintings (most of them starkly realistic portraits of Russian farm girls and of staunch, weathered Russian mothers defending their children against hard, ugly brutish German troops), a room dedicated to pictures and models of the performances of the Bolshoi Ballet and the Moscow State Orchestra, and a room full of baskets and rugs made by Russian peasants, labeled *Salon d'Ouvrages Soviétiques.*

As impressive as the factories and machines were, when we poked around from booth to exhibit we were struck by two lacks: first, a lack of originality. The cameras were obvious copies from the German, the watches from the Swiss; the television sets could have had Westinghouse labels on them; and what few machines we recognized displayed nothing new, but were simply new models of the basic tools of industry. The one item of striking originality was, of course, the space capsule.

The second lack was of any displays, save a few black and white photographs, showing how the Russian people lived. There was no mockup of the average middle-class apartment, no exhibition of any facilities for leisure time, no indication of any standard of living whatsoever. The impression one got was of being subjected to endless and clumsy propaganda. It was annoying, for the exhibition could have been fascinating.

We decided to leave, and we started to walk toward the door. "Just a second," I said. "This is absurd. If we came all the way out here, we might as well get something out of it."

"Like what?" said Bob.

"Like talking to a Russian."

"About what? The New York Yankees?"

"I don't know. Anything. Just see what they're like."

"Any Russian in particular?" said Bob. "Or just any Russian?"

I looked around at the booths. "There's one who's not doing anything," I said, pointing toward a booth. "Let's see what he has to say."

"You go ahead," said Bob. "I'm going to the restaurant upstairs to get a sandwich. I'll meet you there."

The Russian was alone at the booth. The device he was assigned to explain was a big optical something-or-other, and the public was not showing great interest, so he wasn't busy. He sat at a small wooden table reading *l'Humanité*, the French Communist newspaper. He was of medium build with curly blond hair, and he wore tiny, perfectly round, rimless spectacles. He could have been no more than twenty-five.

I had made up a question about the exposition as an excuse for speaking to him. "Pardon me," I said in French, "could I ask you a question?"

The Russian looked up at me. He smiled, and his round face and bright blue eyes were friendly. "Of course," he said.

"I've just been through the exposition, and I wondered if there was any room that showed more about the actual life in Russia."

"No," he said. "It's too bad, in a way, because for someone not technically minded, I guess the exposition is dull. Was there anything specific you wanted to see?"

"No, nothing in particular."

"You're American?"

"Yes."

"I saw your American newspaper. May I look?"

I handed him the copy of the Paris edition of the *New*

York Herald Tribune that I'd been carrying under my arm. "Will you sit down?" he said. "My English is not good, and I would like to practice with you for a moment."

I sat down and offered him a cigarette. "Ah," he said, "an American cigarette. I will, thank you. These French things are going to kill me one day."

For five minutes or so we read passages from the paper aloud. "You see?" he said. "My English is not good."

"It's a good deal better than my Russian."

"You speak no Russian?"

"Not a word."

He nodded. "I hear it is a hard language for foreigners to learn."

There was a pause. "Do you enjoy working at the exposition?" I asked.

"It's not bad. I enjoy being in Paris. The work is not very interesting, but some of the people you meet are. And I do get to see some pretty girls. *La!*" He shook his hand up and down in the French gesture of appreciation.

"Have you been out with any of them?"

"No. I haven't asked any. Anyway, I don't think I'd be permitted to go out with one."

"Why not?"

"I don't know. Just the rules, I guess. Maybe I would. As I said, I haven't tried yet. I may get up my courage and ask one." He added, "If I'm allowed to."

A woman stopped at the booth to ask directions. When she had gone, he said, "May we read some more from your paper?" We spread the paper on the desk. As he began to read, I noticed two Frenchmen standing silently by the rail of the booth. They didn't seem to want anything, but were just listening to our conversation.

"What's this?" said the Russian, indicating a paragraph in the paper. "I'm not sure I understand it. Please tell me what it says."

I looked at the piece. "It says that an African delegate to the U.N. was beaten up by thugs in Central Park in New York."

"But that's not true."

"I'm afraid it is."

"No, no, you misunderstand me. I know he was beaten up, but it was not by thugs. He was beaten up by the police."

"Where do you get that?"

"Here," he said. He reached under the desk and pulled out a copy of *Pravda*. He read from an article on the front page, translating into French. "You see?" he said. "It says he was beaten up by the police."

"I'm afraid that's wrong." I looked around, and the two people at the rail had suddenly become six, all standing quietly, listening.

"But no," said the Russian. "*Your* paper is wrong."

"How can you be sure?"

"I know it, that's all. In your paper is a lie."

"And there's no chance that your paper could have made a slight error?"

"None."

"I see," I said. "Well, I didn't come here to fight with you, so let's drop it."

"Fine," he said. He turned to the ten people who by now had gathered at the rail. "May I help you?" he asked.

"No," said one of the men.

We went back to the paper. "Here's another thing," said the Russian. "It says here that a boy was shot yesterday at the Berlin wall. Where does your paper get such information?"

"From a reporter who was there," I said.

"But it is a lie!"

"It seems to have happened."

"Well, I know nothing about it."

"It's right there in front of you."

"In *your* paper, yes. But I know nothing about it."

One of the men at the rail said, "It happened."

"No," said the Russian. "It didn't."

"Do you mean," I said, "that just because it wasn't in your paper, it didn't happen?"

"Yes."

"So for you, all that exists, all reality, consists of what your government tells you. What about the things your papers and your government don't tell you? Do they simply not exist? I mean, even unimportant things."

The Russian looked at the ever-growing crowd at the rail. "I cannot answer that," he said, softly.

Another man in the crowd spoke up. "What would happen in Russia if someone openly disagreed with the government? Or with the papers? It's all the same."

"No one does," said the Russian.

"You mean everyone agrees with everything the government says?"

"Yes."

"That includes you?" I said.

"Of course."

"What about the rule on going out with girls while you're here?" I asked. "Do you agree with that, too?"

He smiled faintly. "I'm sure it is the best thing."

"It's a shame if there are no differences of opinion," I said. "If the government controls all means of informing the public, the public will be misinformed. The people lose all their power."

He did not reply. He looked at the group standing at the rail. There were easily twenty-five people listening to us. Suddenly it occurred to me that I had unwittingly gotten myself into the position of having to defend my country in front of an audience. I was sure the same thing had occurred to the Russian, and I knew he had the advantage. His French was better than mine, and it came to him more easily than mine to me. Also, I was certain that he had been well briefed before being let out of Russia, his arguments reinforced with technicalities, treaties, declarations, and agreements that he could summon forth, sure in the knowledge that the average layman would have no documented counter to them. If I had been George Kennan, I might have stood a chance. As Peter Benchley, I was in a hole, and I was scared. I felt like an actor who knows he has forgotten his lines and waits in terror for his cue.

I was thinking of feigning illness or otherwise stopping the discussion when suddenly a man in the rear of the crowd yelled, "Murderer! In Hungary you killed people, and now in Germany you kill people."

The Russian paled, and his face got red with anger. When he spoke, his voice was low, controlled. "I know nothing of what you are talking about."

I decided to try to keep him on principle, away from my Achilles' heel, technicalities. "Wait," I said. "Granting for a moment that none of this happened, could you explain it if it did happen?"

"Of course," he said. "You see, to us the state is far more important than any individual, and therefore individuals or, if you will, groups of individuals, have to be completely subservient to the will of the state."

"And this theory, or doctrine, justifies killing hordes of people in Germany?"

He snapped at me, "Why must you continually bring up Germany? Whatever happens there is not our affair. It is the affair of the German Democratic Republic. We do not now, nor have we ever, interfered in the internal affairs of a sovereign nation."

The hue and cry at that remark stopped all conversation. Again, the Russian was furious. "You Americans get very self-righteous about Berlin," he said. "You speak of the shame of a divided country. Don't you realize that it was the Soviet Union that fought for a united Germany, and that it was the British who finally provoked the separation into two Germanies?"

"Oh?" I said.

"Yes. They were the first to institute a separate currency, and they were the ones who broke away from the central government and began to hold separate administrative councils in West Berlin, in places where no administrative councils had ever been held before. What do you say to that?"

"I'm afraid I can't say anything."

I was searching desperately for an avenue of escape when he struck again. "You have, of course, read the declarations of the Allies for the control of Berlin, no?"

"Not recently," I said, choking on the words.

"Then the Potsdam Agreement?"

"Not in years."

"In all these documents, the main point of agreement between the four powers was the complete extirpation of German militarism and Nazism. A simple point to agree on, don't you think?"

"Simple," I said.

"And yet of the four governments, only the Soviet Union has adhered to this agreement. It is in the West zone that the revanchists and Nazis still meet and plot subversion. It

is from the West that all the trouble comes. It is only the
Soviet Union that prevents war. The Germans *want* war."

"Oh, now please! Don't you think it's silly to say that
any people *want* war?"

"So you think. You can complain to us about stopping
one spy from escaping—"

"So you admit it!"

"No! It is hypothetical. You complain because we try
to guarantee the security and sovereignty of the DDR, and
yet the German militarists create such groups as the so-called
'Fighting Group Against Inhumanity' in 1949, and you con-
done it completely."

"The what?" I said, weakly. I was helpless, and none of
the people in the crowd seemed to know any more than I.
There was silence, except for the occasional clearing of a
throat and now and again the wonderful French expression
of frustration, a *"Mais . . ."* that trails off into a whisper.

The Russian smiled. He took off his glasses and wiped the
sweat from his eyebrows and nose. "You talk about our press
and say we never hear the truth. What about yours? You
have never heard of the Fighting Group Against Inhumanity?"

"No."

"It was a group of revanchists whose sole aim it was to
undermine the government of the DDR. In 1949 the group
made raids on the S-Bahn and set many carriages on fire and
damaged a number of construction sites. Your government
did nothing. I could tell you of many other incidents, war
propaganda, spy tunnels—"

"I'm sure you could," I said. My ears were hot, and my
collar felt too tight. I looked at the crowd. People were
jammed together on all sides of the booth. The Russian
looked, too, and he was nervous. "Let me ask you one more

question," I said, in a last-ditch attempt to redeem myself.
"How can you yourself, as an indi—no, you don't recognize
the individual—as a human being, then. As a human being,
how can you justify the forced confinement of hundreds of
thousands of people?"

He waited for a moment, looking at the crowd. Then he
said, "Do Americans have to have a visa to travel in France?"

"Only if they stay more than three months."

"Do Frenchmen have to have a visa to travel in America?"

"Yes."

"You see?" he said. "It's the same thing."

"It's *what?* How can you say—"

"I must go now," he said. "It has been interesting."
Abruptly, he stood up and walked away into the crowd by
the space capsule.

I sat at the table, trying to understand his last statement.
In a few minutes, the crowd had dispersed, and I folded my
paper and got up to go. As I left the booth, I saw the Russian
standing alone under the airplane display platform, smoking
a cigarette. He beckoned to me, and I went over.

"I wanted to apologize for stopping the discussion that
way," he said. "It is not a good thing to do. But the crowd
was beginning to make me nervous, and I didn't know what
they were going to do. There were a great many people there,
you know."

"I know," I said. "I can't blame you."

"The French are a volatile people. A riot would not have
helped matters."

"No."

Bob, who had spotted us as he came down the stairs, joined
us under the platform. I introduced him to the Russian,
who said his name was Mikhail.

"What time do you get off work?" I asked.

"In about half an hour," said Mikhail.

"Would you like to have a drink with us across the street? There's a café nearby."

He thought for a moment. "I would like that," he said. "I will meet you there in about forty minutes."

Bob and I went to the café, and Mikhail joined us when he was through work. He didn't know what to drink, so we ordered him scotch. We stayed in the café, the three of us, until after dark, talking about French girls, Russian girls, American girls, Coney Island, Chicago, Moscow, and Louis Armstrong.

7

IN NOVEMBER, about two weeks before I was to leave again for Spain, where I was going to spend Christmas, Bob and I decided to go to Berlin for a weekend. The infamous Wall had been erected in August, and since it was a personal concern of ours, *in re* not only the world situation but also our draft status, Bob and I thought we should see it.

I had some friends who were living in Berlin, Mr. and Mrs. Arthur Potter. Mr. Potter is Berlin correspondent for an American newspaper, and though I was sure he would be too busy to see us, I sent him a telegram saying we were coming and would appreciate it if he would give us even a few minutes. I received a charming reply, offering to lodge and feed us for as long as we could stay.

We didn't know how to get to Berlin. We knew we could

fly, but the plane fare was too expensive for us. Besides, we thought we should see something of East Germany on the way. We had heard that one had to get a visa from the East Germans before entering East Germany, but East Germany had no embassy or consulate in Paris. And we didn't know whether the visa requirement was for trains or cars or both. I called the American Embassy and asked if they could tell me how to get a visa to East Germany.

"Why do you want to go to Berlin?" said the man who answered the phone.

"To see it," I said.

"As tourists?"

"Yes."

"I'd suggest that you forget it," said the man.

"Why?"

"It's just not a good idea to go, that's all."

"Is it dangerous?"

"Not exactly, no. It's just not a good idea."

"Is there a State Department rule against it?"

"No."

"If we did go, would we be allowed to show our passports to the East Germans?"

"Allowed by whom?"

"By the U.S. I know diplomats can't, or won't, show their passports to the East Germans."

"There's no rule against it."

"Then would you please tell me how to go about getting the visa?"

"I don't know." He hung up.

Our apartment was less than a block from the Russian Embassy, so one afternoon I went there to ask about the visa. I was admitted by a short, nervous, brisk man who showed me into a waiting room. In about five minutes, a large, burly man came in and asked if he could help me.

"I'd like to find out about getting a visa to East Germany," I said.

"That's not our affair," said the man.

"I know you don't issue the visas, but could you tell me how to get one? Or at least if I need one?"

"You must see the representatives of the German Democratic Republic," he said.

"They have no legation in Paris."

"I know."

"Then what do I do?"

"Go to the Bulgarian consulate." He turned and walked out of the room.

The Bulgarians said they didn't know anything about visas to East Germany. Bob and I decided we would get on a train and go, the hell with the visa. If they turned us back at the border, we would fly.

We got on the train late Thursday afternoon, and spent a miserable night hunched over on hard, sloping banquettes in an unheated second-class compartment. My only coat was a light raincoat, and I used it for a different purpose every hour—first as a pillow, then as a footrest, then for whatever slight warmth it could give me. Early Friday morning we changed trains, deep in West Germany, and at noon we approached the border. The countryside was bare, spotted with an occasional farm, one or two small towns, and a few trees.

At twelve-twenty, the train stopped. Blue-uniformed troops got on and began stamping passports with the exit stamp from West Germany. The faceless official stamped our passports without a word. The train moved on for another five minutes, then stopped again. We could see two gatehouses and the beginning of lines of barbed wire that stretched away into the distance. Four men in green uniforms came into our car. They were young, and they wore high black boots. Two of them carried Russian submachine guns. They worked in pairs, two on each side of the car, stamping passports. Most of the people on the train were Berliners returning home, and the troops stamped their passports automatically, checking the picture against the face of the traveler, hitting the passport once with the heavy green stamp.

When they came to us, one of them took my passport, the other took Bob's. They both started to stamp them, then stopped, almost simultaneously. The soldier who had my passport was, I estimated, no more than twenty-one. His face was fleshy, with round red cheeks, and his long blond hair stuck out from under the back of his cap. "Amerikaner," he said. He stared at me, at my face, my hair, my clothes, my shoes. Then he turned to his companion, who was staring at Bob, and said something. The other soldier shrugged his shoulders. They exchanged a few more words, then turned to us. "Visa," said the one with my passport.

"I haven't got one," I said.

He didn't understand me, so I spread my hands in a gesture of emptiness, and shook my head.

"Visa," he said to Bob.

"Nope," said Bob.

A woman sitting in the seat opposite ours said, "I can help?"

I explained our problem, and she said something to the soldiers. They spoke to her, then turned and left the car, still holding our passports.

"What to do," said the woman. "Don't know Americans.

No visa." She was about forty, short and very thin, with gnarled, bony hands that looked much older than her years.

I asked what the soldiers were doing.

"Get another man," she said.

The soldiers reappeared, followed by a stout, elderly official with gold-rimmed glasses. They stopped at our seat, and the official clicked his heels together and gave us a quick bow. "Please," he said.

"Thank you," said Bob.

"You have no visas?"

We said we didn't.

"You will buy visas, please." He took a pad from his pocket and began to copy information from our passports.

"Will you take French francs?" I asked.

"You have no West marks?"

"No."

"Very well. French francs will do. Ten new francs each."

We gave him the money, the equivalent of two dollars, and he stamped our passports. He clicked his heels, bowed, and left.

The soldiers remained by our seat. They spoke to each other in whispers, glancing at us. They seemed to be arguing.

The woman leaned over to me and said, "They don't know. One wishes speak to you. Other say no good."

I held a package of cigarettes out to the soldiers. The one who had had my passport reached tentatively to take a cigarette. His friend grabbed his arm and snapped at him. He smiled a quick, apologetic smile, and followed his friend out of the car.

The train began to move, and Bob and I pressed our faces against the window. To both sides of the train there was barbed wire. Barbed wire, then ditches, then more barbed wire. The countryside was gray and brown—gray where the cold fall had killed the grass, brown where the land had been gouged away to make the ditches. Every mile or two, we passed a pair of guards walking up and down by the wire. They carried submachine guns, and one pair we saw had a dog.

The woman stared silently out the window for more than an hour. Finally, as we were pulling away from a stop, she spoke. "Here there is no life," she said. "In the East zone nobody on the streets." She waved her hand at the deserted streets of a small village. "I don't know where the people is," she said. "The people is gone."

We arrived in Berlin late that afternoon and went immediately to the Potters' house. The house is on the outskirts of the city, in the American sector. It is a modern house, comfortably furnished, and behind it are acres of grass and trees that slope gradually down toward a river. We put our bags upstairs and joined the Potters in the living room. A butler brought us a drink. Mr. Potter introduced him to us as Hans.

"Hans is an interesting guy," said Mr. Potter. "See if you get to talk to him while you're here. He's on the list of most wanted defectors from East Berlin. He got out a few months ago, and while any other German can go back into East Berlin for a visit, if Hans ever crossed the border, they'd grab him immediately."

I said, "Do you mean they have the name of every wanted man at every border post?"

"There are certain crossing points for certain nationalities," said Mr. Potter, "and at the German points they have all the names of wanted Germans, yes. They have a big book, and as you go through the checkpoint, they take your passport, pass it through a window to a man who has the book, and if your name is in it, you never get your passport back. They take you away. Your official listing in the West thereafter would be 'missing.' "

Since the next day was Saturday, Mr. Potter didn't have to work, and he offered to spend the day showing us West Berlin. He said we would have to see East Berlin on our own, since for him, an American newspaperman, to go into East Berlin was, depending on the mood of the East Germans at the time, at best unwise and at worst impossible.

We awoke early, had breakfast, and drove to the center of West Berlin. We parked the car and walked down the Kurfürstendamm, the main street, which looked like a modern Champs Elysées. It is a wide street, gleaming with new restaurants, hotels, cafés, and stores. The neon lights, though not as subdued as the soft pinks and blues on the Champs Elysées, were attractive, not gaudy, when set against the shiny newness of the buildings. The street was as crowded as Fifth Avenue at noon, and people talked and gestured and laughed and window-shopped and sat in cafés. We sensed a great feeling of life, and we could see none of the fear that we had read held Berlin in a tight grip. I mentioned this seeming lack of concern to Mr. Potter.

"It's really not as carefree as it appears, nor as grim as what you've heard," said Mr. Potter. "To a certain extent, the carefree attitude is a defense mechanism. They can't think about the Wall and the Reds all the time, or they'd go nuts, so they force themselves to be gayer than they normally would. It helps them forget. On the other hand, they're a hell of a lot more confident, more happy, and more secure than the papers tell you. Read some of these papers long enough and you'll think the people are about to commit mass suicide."

On the Kurfürstendamm, and on the streets nearby, you

can buy clothes and food from anywhere in the world. There
are French shoes, American shirts, British woolens, Chinese
silks. And though the restaurants are mostly German, showing knackwurst, bratwurst, veal, steak, and pastry in the
windows, American, Japanese, and Italian foods are readily
available.

We window-shopped for almost an hour, and then Mr.
Potter led us back to the car. "I'll start by showing you
what the Wall is like out of town," he said. "In a way, it's
more dramatic there." We drove for about fifteen minutes,
through Berlin and then through the wooded outskirts.
Suddenly the pavement stopped, and we saw a cinder-block
wall, perhaps five feet tall, topped by two rows of barbed
wire, one leaning toward us, the other leaning away. Mr.
Potter parked the car in a dirt turn-around, and we got out.

The wall was not straight, but followed the border exactly,
twisting through the woods. We walked along it for fifty
or sixty yards. "Look there," said Mr. Potter. We drew
back from the wall, and over the top we could see a house
some ten yards away. The house stood in the East sector,
its back door not five yards from the wall. "Now come here."
We followed Mr. Potter to a spot directly across the wall
from the back door of the house. "Look where you're standing," he said.

I looked down and saw that I was standing on a row of
dead flowers. "This is the man's garden," said Mr. Potter.
"This whole area." I could see the remains of the small
stone fence the man had erected to mark his property. The
wall cut the property in half, separating the house from
almost all its land .

"Did they *have* to do it this way?" I said.

Mr. Potter nodded. "Sure," he said. "If they let the man

keep his garden, they'd have had to build the wall on American territory. They do things precisely."

"Then why doesn't he leave?" asked Bob. "He could get over the wall right here. I don't see any guards."

"He probably could," said Mr. Potter. "There are guards, but they make regular rounds, and the chances are he could make it. But he'd have to leave all his property—his house, his furniture, everything. Would you do it?"

"I don't know," said Bob. "I think so, if I were young enough."

"That's another point. He's almost certainly an old man, or at least in his fifties. They're sure it wouldn't be worth it to him. If he were a young man, they'd have moved him out of there long ago."

We drove back into town and had lunch at a café on the Kurfürstendamm. After lunch, Mr. Potter said we were going to Bernauerstrasse, in the French sector. "This is the place you've seen in all the papers," he said. "This is what the world knows as the Wall. And rightly, I guess. It's the most horrible."

Bernauerstrasse is the street split by the Wall. The border runs along the fronts of apartment buildings, and the windows and doors have been bricked off, the inhabitants moved deeper into East Berlin. There are crosses on the sidewalk to mark where people have tried to escape and have died from falling to the pavement or from being shot as they shinnied down a drainpipe or lowered themselves by ropes from the roofs. One of the crosses is wrapped in barbed wire, and a pot of flowers rests at its base. At one point on the street, a church is set back twenty yards or so from the wall. It is closed, and its congregation now attends a church more than a mile away. Since there is no building in front of the church, there is a space between two apartment houses where the wall is low. The East German police, the Vopos, used to stand on platforms behind the wall, from which they could get a full view of people trying to escape from buildings up and down the street. When the West Berliners discovered this, they erected two huge cardboard barriers jutting out from the buildings toward the street. Now the Vopos have no view at all.

When we were in the open space between the cardboard barriers, we looked down into East Berlin. Half a block into East Berlin, a young man leaned out a window and raised his arm at us.

"What's he doing?" I said. "Waving?"

"I don't think so," said Mr. Potter. "He's giving us the Communist salute. He's mocking us."

"But he can't be. Look, he's waving his arm."

"Yes, but his fist is clenched and . . ." Mr. Potter stopped. "Do you want to believe that he's waving?"

"Yes."

"Okay, he's waving."

We continued down the street, walking on the sidewalk and peering at the bricked windows and doors, trying to see inside. Suddenly a policeman ran up to Mr. Potter, gave him a courtesy salute, and began speaking excitedly in German. Mr. Potter said something, and the policeman crossed to the other side of the street.

Mr. Potter turned to us. "We'll have to get off this side of the street."

"Why?" asked Bob.

"The police don't like to have people walk on this side. There's always a chance we'll get shot, and—"

"Shot! You mean they'd just lean over the wall and *shoot* us, here in West territory?"

"They've done it, and then claimed you were walking in their territory. Technically, they're right. This sidewalk, or part of it, is in East Berlin. But the real danger isn't from bullets. It's from bricks. That's their favorite."

"How do you mean?" said Bob.

"When the Wall first went up, a number of people were killed along here by bricks which 'dislodged' themselves from rooftops and fell on their heads. There's no way to prove that the brick didn't just fall. Of course, a red brick falling from a gray building is a little strange, but still, there's no proof."

We hurried to the other side of the street, and walked back to the car. "Now we'll go look at some Nazi ruins," said Mr. Potter. "We'll see as much as we can today, so you can spend tomorrow in East Berlin."

The next morning, a cab came for us at ten o'clock. The driver was told to drop us at Friedrichstrasse, a block away from the American checkpoint, Checkpoint Charlie. Bob debated taking his camera, then decided to leave it, since he knew that taking photographs was illegal in most of East Berlin, and he was not anxious to lose his camera. Or, for that matter, to be arrested.

We asked the driver to take us past the canals, for Mr. Potter had told us that on Sundays one could get a better sense of what the Wall meant to the German people, and the canals were where the people met. We stopped near one, and Bob and I got out. Crowds of people stood on the bank, waving balloons, handkerchiefs, and pieces of colored cloth at the eastern shore. A young couple had tied red balloons on the ends of sticks and were waving them back and forth over their heads. An old woman waved a handkerchief in a halfhearted, weary gesture, and from time to time she dabbed her eyes with it. A man held a child on his shoulders, and the child bounced happily up and down, clapping his hands.

Across the canal, the Vopos had planted high hedges and put up four strands of barbed wire, so no one could get close enough to see the waving. Guards patrolled the wire to keep people moving and to stop crowds from gathering at the spaces between the hedges. In a window of one of the buildings a hundred yards or so back from the canal, someone appeared wearing a red shirt. He stayed at the window only a moment, then disappeared.

On the way to the checkpoint, we drove down the Kurfürstendamm. The cafés were jammed with people drinking coffee and Coca-Cola and beer, reading the papers or talking and laughing with one another. The sun sparkled on the new buildings, giving the whole street an aura of gold.

Before the border was closed, Friedrichstrasse was like any other street in Berlin. It consisted of blocks of stores and apartment houses, some in East Berlin, some in West Berlin. When the Wall went up, things changed. Now an American guardhouse stands in the middle of the street by the border. It is surrounded by sandbag barricades, manned at all times by two or three soldiers. The rest of the troops, and the tanks, are stationed less than a block behind the border. The houses directly on the border have been evacuated. The apartment house on the left, facing East Berlin, has no windows, only sandbags which support the barrel of a heavy machine gun.

The East Germans, always alert to prevent escapes, had leveled their side of the checkpoint and set up flags where buildings used to be. The only building they left was one small house just across the line from the windowless house in the American sector. They use this house for their checkpoint.

West German police and American soldiers were milling around the American guardhouse as we went in. An American sergeant in battle dress took our passports and wrote down our names and numbers. He asked us when we planned to return to the West, and we said two o'clock. That gave us three hours to wander on foot through East Berlin. He noted the time of departure and the estimated time of arrival in a big notebook, and said, "Don't be too late, or we'll have to start looking for you over there."

We left the guardhouse and walked the fifty yards to the East German checkpoint. A green-uniformed Vopo stopped us in front of the building. "Your passport," he said, and we handed him our passports. He passed them through a slit cut in a drawn window shade, and suddenly I experienced a slight sinking feeling, a feeling of helplessness. I remembered Mr. Potter's remarks about Hans, and I had a picture of a little man with a blackjack dealer's eyeshade, poring over a huge ledger looking for my name among hundreds of "wanted" names in the American community. Then, through the slit, the passport was handed back.

The first large street we came to was Unter den Linden, which used to be the main street of East Berlin. We stopped on a corner and looked up and down the street. "You remember that woman on the train?" said Bob. " 'I don't know where the people is. The people is gone.' " On the whole street we could see three people. They were not dawdling, not stopping to chat. They walked with their heads down, and they walked fast.

We walked on, looking in shop windows. In a meat

market, one lone string of sausage hung in the window. The rest of the hooks were empty. We put our faces to the window and looked at the cases inside. We could see two trays of pig's knuckles, and two more strings of sausage. I remembered what someone had told me about East Berlin. The phrase in markets, he said, was not "I will have . . ." but "Do you by any chance have . . .?" An East German girl he knew had gone into a meat market one day and asked if there was any stewmeat.

"Of course," said the butcher, and he took a piece of red meat from a hook on the wall and hacked off a piece.

The next day she went back to the market and asked if there were any cuts of good beefsteak.

"Of course," said the butcher, and he took the same piece of meat from the same hook and cut her a slice from the same end.

As we walked along, I began to feel uneasy. There was something different about East Berlin, aside from the lack of people, and I couldn't put my finger on what it was. There was less traffic than in West Berlin, and less of a variety of makes of cars, but that wasn't it. Nor was it the fact that there was not an excessive number of policemen about. Suddenly Bob discovered what it was.

"Hey," he said, looking up. "Is the sun still shining?"

The sun was indeed still shining, and there were no clouds in the sky, yet the whole atmosphere was that of a cloudy, dreary day. There was no color. Nothing shone, nothing glittered. There were no whites to reflect the sun and gleam in your eye, no yellows to draw your attention, no greens or blues or pinks to bring the city to life. There were only two colors, gray and reddish gray—gray in the buildings that were standing, reddish gray in the charred ruins of the bombed-out areas that no one had repaired. The government had made one attempt to atone for this lack of color: on the side of perhaps one building every two or three blocks they had hung red propaganda banners. "Western Revanchists Must Go." "Berlin—Free City." "The Only Wish of the DDR Is Peace."

We walked past the university, past the ruins of the old Reichstag, and came eventually to the showplace of East Berlin, Karl Marx Allee, whose name, before the recent change of heart, had been Stalinallee. It was here that Bob and I both wished he had brought his camera. The buildings, all of them new, were only one deep on each side of the street. They were an off-white gray, and the oldest of them were already sorely in need of repair. But as drab as they were, they stood like castles before the debris and tenements nearby.

"What do you call that style?" said Bob. "Neo-Communist austere?"

Some of the buildings on Karl Marx Allee were not finished, but were only façades, and though they looked respectable enough from the street in front, from a distance they looked like stage sets.

We were hungry, and we thought of getting something to hold us until we crossed back into West Berlin. There were no restaurants in sight, and we didn't remember having seen any so far, but going on the theory that even Communists have to eat, we assumed there was a restaurant somewhere. Suddenly it occurred to us that we had no East German money, and we knew that East Germans were not allowed to accept West marks. We had been warned against buying any East marks at the border, for the government of the Deutsche Demokratische Republik had established a one-for-one exchange rate that was totally unrealistic. An East mark was worth approximately one-fifth of a West mark, so for a dollar we would get in exchange only twenty cents. Not only would we lose on the exchange, we had been told, but all our East marks would be confiscated before we left, and we would be given nothing in return. The East Germans wanted hard currencies, and they couldn't afford to let their own currency get out of the country and be held by another government as trade credit. We decided not to eat.

We walked farther, through the dark, empty streets, until we saw a sign on a building in French, English, and German that said there was an exhibition inside that gave the history of the DDR in pictures. We went in and spent half an hour looking at photographs of Nazi brutalities and at East German editorial cartoons excoriating the West. The stock character representing the West was a fat man in a top hat, tailcoat, and striped pants. He had saw teeth and long claws, and he was invariably gobbling up the poor, raggedy, sad-eyed peasants. In the next box he was being stabbed in the rear by a pitchfork held by the same peasants, who were now firm-jawed, clean-cut, and hard-muscled.

When we left the exhibition, we walked back toward the border, for it was after one, and we did not want to be late and perhaps cause an incident. At the border, we did not pass through as easily as on the way in. We were ushered into a small room, where a thin, mustachioed man sat behind a desk. A Vopo stood beside him. The man nodded, and the Vopo took our passports and passed them through an opening in the wall. The thin man stood up.

"Have you got any East marks?" he said.

"No," said Bob. I shook my head.

"Take off your coats. Have you got any East marks?"

We both said we didn't have any East marks. We took off our raincoats.

"Take off your jackets," said the man, as he put his hand in the pocket of my raincoat. "Are you sure you have no East marks?"

"I'm sure," I said.

He went through our jacket pockets. "Turn out your trouser pockets," he said. "Empty your wallets." We did as we were told, dumping the contents of our pockets on his desk. The man looked at Bob's pants pockets. He patted Bob's shirt pocket, and there was the sound of paper crumpling. "What have we here?" he said, smiling. He reached into Bob's shirt pocket and pulled out a package of cigarettes. The smile died on his face.

"Pall Mall," said Bob. "Outstanding—and, they are mild."

"You can go," said the man. He reached through the hole in the wall and brought out our passports. He threw them on the desk.

We dressed, and went outside. A man with a wide-brim hat and a black overcoat was standing outside the door holding a pile of booklets. "American?" he said.

"Yes," I said.

"Here." He handed us each four booklets, and we put them in our pockets without looking at them.

We took a taxi back to the Potters', and when we were comfortably ensconced in the library, cuddling glasses of strong spirits, we looked at the books. They were standard propaganda literature, most of them quite dull. One book, however, called *A Central Problem*, had photographs, some apparently doctored, some real, some presented out of context, and there was a text accompanying and explaining each picture. A few of its more spectacular passages follow:

Along with the separate currency reform and the division
of the city some Western politicians provoked the so-called
"Berlin crisis," and installed the "air lift." The "Berlin
Crisis" was engineered by them in order to distract attention
from their policy of dividing Germany and Berlin. At the
same time it contributed to creating the "front-line city atmosphere" which the German reactionaries and the Western
powers need for their bridgehead policy.

Crime statistics in West Berlin also illustrate the effects of
systematic front-line policy propaganda. About two hundred
crimes are committed every day in West Berlin. The number of young people sentenced in court increased from 2,999
in 1954 to 5,939 in 1957. The proportion of suicides is also
higher in West Berlin than in any other city in the world.
[Author's note: that figure is accurate—for cities. In 1959
West Berlin's suicide rate was 39 for every 100,000 people.
However, East Germany's suicide rate of 28 per 100,000 was
in that year the highest of any *country* in the world. Ex-
cluding West Berlin, West Germany's suicide rate was 18.7
per 100,000. The above are World Health Organization figures that appeared in the *New York Times* in January, 1962.]

The security measures taken on the borders of West Berlin
[the construction of the Wall] on August 13, 1961, by the
government of the German Democratic Republic, in agreement with the Governments of the Warsaw Pact States, do
not affect the regulations for traffic and supervision on the
communications between West Berlin and West Germany.
These measures to maintain peace and to protect the German Democratic Republic, particularly its capital, Berlin,
and to ensure the security of other socialist states, remain in
force until the conclusion of a German peace treaty.

We left for Paris the next afternoon. While we were waiting for a cab to come for us, we showed Mr. and Mrs. Potter the propaganda books we had been handed at the border. Mr. Potter leafed through *A Central Problem,* and set it down on the coffee table. "You know," he said, "as funny and absurd as this stuff seems to anyone who knows better, there's a lot of danger in it. The danger is for the young people, and it gets worse each day. Every day more people die who knew other values and remembered other times, times when a system wasn't forced on them. And every day more people are born who can't know anything but what's told to them by their government. As long as some of the people who remember are alive, there's always a possibility— slim, I'll grant you, but still a possibility—that they'll rise up and do something about it. But the possibility is made slimmer with every death and every birth. Physiologically, the exchange is balanced, one for one. Ideologically, it's grossly unbalanced. It's the death of a free mind and the birth of a mind that will never be free."

The cab arrived, and Bob and I thanked Mr. and Mrs. Potter and drove off to the station. As we crossed the East German border for the last time, I looked out the window and saw a group of the blue-suited Communist youth corps marching in formation. Not one of the children looked more than sixteen.

8

WE SPENT my last weekend in France with a friend, at his family's house on the Loire. It was to be a partridge-shooting wine-tasting weekend, but the latter took precedence over the former, and all pretensions about hunting were dropped when I shot a seventy-five foot barn.

I sold the Peugeot in the beginning of December, after two costly trips to the casinos at Forge les Eaux and Enghien-les-Bains where I tried to play James Bond and break the table at chemin de fer. Once I wore a single black glove, thinking that luck might smile on such a man of mystery. Smersh won out every time, however, and I threw my glove away in dismal defeat. Had I been in the area, I would have cast it into the Bosporus. As it was, I was forced to settle for the Seine.

I left Paris on the 19th of December. Bob was at school. I left him a note and some money to cover my half of December's rent, and took a cab to the station. It was a cloudless day, with a deep blue winter sky, and as I rode down the Quai St. Michel, I looked across the river and saw the sunlight dancing off the water and soaking the houses on the right bank in a white-gold glow. It was a sharper color than I had seen as I flew in in July, for now the air was crisp and cold and gave none of the shimmering softness that heat gives to sunlight. I spoke aloud the last line of "La Seine," ". . . car la Seine est une amante, et son amant c'est Paris." The cab driver turned and looked at me as though he thought I had taken leave of my senses.

I spent two leisurely weeks in Madrid with some friends of my parents. Then, in the beginning of January, when the cold in Spain had become unbearable, I went south to Algeciras, across the bay from Gibraltar, to wait for the *Saturnia,* on which my parents were sailing to Naples. I bought a tourist-class ticket for the voyage from Gibraltar to Naples. The ticket cost $38 and was, minute for minute and mile for mile, the cheapest traveling I had done.

For the next four weeks I played the happy tourist. I went sightseeing with my parents in Rome, grew fat on Italian food, went sightseeing with my parents in Athens, grew thin on Greek food, flew back to Rome and saw St. Peter's tomb, and got fat again on Italian food.

On the 10th of February, I flew from Rome to Cairo, hoping that Charlie Ravenel had somehow managed to get there too. Months earlier, we had agreed to meet at the Nile Hilton Hotel, the only landmark in Cairo that we both knew. The plane left in the late afternoon, and as it flew southeast

across the Mediterranean, I could see the sun move down in
the sky. First the sky was blue, then dark blue, then navy
blue as the sun settled for a moment on the horizon, a red
ball, squat and glowing. Then all at once it disappeared, and
the plane flew on in darkness.

During the flight, I thought of what I was about to throw
myself into. I was prepared, I believed, for new places, new
customs, and new people. I had considered how new and
how different life in the East would be, and though I had
never known real discomfort or squalor or dirt or heat, for
some reason the prospects didn't bother me. I was excited
rather than worried, curious rather than afraid.

What I was not sure of was how I would get along with
Ravenel. For the first week or two, Bob and I had had to
exert a great effort to be patient with each other, to learn
about and try to understand each other. I had known Bob
in college and for a year had even roomed in the same suite
with him. But we had never lived in close quarters, and
neither of us, it turned out, was just peaches and cream. But
within a short time, perhaps because of our many similarities,
perhaps even because of our differences, we settled down to
a fine understanding. There were never any serious clashes
of personality, just the occasional annoyances caused by two
individuals exercising their day-to-day quirks and manner-
isms. On the whole, we got along superbly.

With Charles DuFort Ravenel, things might be different.
When Charlie was a senior in high school in Charleston,
South Carolina, he won a Newsboy Scholarship to Exeter,
where he went for one postgraduate year before college. I
met Charlie at Exeter and saw him in classes and exams and
when we studied European history together. Our conversations seldom left the topic of study, and by the end of my
senior year, I knew him only slightly.

At Harvard, Charlie was the savior of what had for years been a mediocre football team. A thinking man's quarterback, he ran, passed, and tackled his way to the status of a household word among Harvard students and alumni. The aura of wonder and admiration was added to by the fact that he is not a large man, standing about five feet nine inches tall and weighing in the neighborhood of a hundred and sixty pounds. The Boston newspapers called him Riverboat, Gaylord, and The Gambler. At one point during his college career, Charlie held five jobs at once, and never did he hold less than two or three. He was a member of the Hasty Pudding and the A.D. Club. And through some feat of supernatural effort and cerebral application, he got good marks. In short, Charlie was a busy lad, and I saw him only rarely. I had dinner with him three or four times, and I saw him at a number of parties. We both lived in Eliot House, so I chatted with him now and then on the paths.

By graduation, when we had tentatively arranged the trip, I knew him, at best, half as well as I knew Bob. We had neither common friends nor, to the best of my knowledge, common interests. I knew him as a friendly, congenial person, whose accomplishments at school showed him to be ambitious, conscientious, and hardworking. And that was all I knew. He could have been a liar, a cheat, a sadist, a back-stabber, a saint, a teetotaler, a bird-lover, or a counterspy for the FBI, and though I suspected he was none of them, I didn't know for sure. On the other hand, he had no way of knowing that *I* was none of the above. So between fits of panic at the incessant banking of the huge flying machine over Cairo airport, I decided that getting to know and learning to put up with one another would be a challenge to us both.

I rode into town on the airport bus and peered out the

window at the Egyptian night. As the houses passed by, my
first reaction was of mild distaste at what instinct recorded
as pseudo- or neo-Arabic architecture. Then suddenly, oh lo
and behold, it occurred to me that this was neither pseudo
nor neo, but honest-to-God Arabic. As we drew nearer Cairo,
neon signs appeared, designed in the beautiful Arabic script.
I began to realize that this was indeed a whole new world,
and all worry about my association with Charlie vanished.
Even if we had not up to now had common interests, they
were going to be thrust upon us by our common adventure
in a strange and fascinating world.

Charlie was already at the Nile Hilton when I arrived.
The hotel fits into the cityscape of Cairo about as well as
Yankee Stadium would. It dominates a wide plaza with
hundreds of feet of glass and concrete that spread in every
direction. The side facing the square is painted with a colos-
sal abstract mural, the modern wildness of which is in-
congruous with its oriental surroundings. The back of the
hotel overlooks the Nile, and on a clear day you can see the
pyramids at Giza from the top floor.

Charlie had been in Jordan and Turkey while I was traveling with my parents, and from a friend in Jordan he had
gotten the names of some people to look up in Cairo. He
called a man early the next morning, and the man asked us
to come see him. We crossed the square and started down
the street toward the man's place of business. Most of the
people on the streets wore white—white robes or white
blouses and white slacks. Egyptian women, unchanged by
years of European influence, still covered their faces with
heavy veils.

We hadn't gone fifty yards when the first shoeshine boy

accosted us. He was young, perhaps ten or twelve. He wore
no shoes, and his only clothing was a pair of tattered, filthy
shorts and a sleeveless T shirt. He came at me from the side.

"Good night, Mike!" he yelled, pulling at my jacket.
"Good night, Mike!"

"No, thank you," I said, and kept walking.

"Good night, Mike!" He held up his shoeshine box. He
tried to move in front of me and block my way. I stepped
around him.

"La! Mishaooz!" said Charlie. The boy looked at him un-
certainly, then laughed.

"What does that mean?" I asked.

"It means 'No, I don't want any.' I learned it from a guy
in Jordan."

"Lot of good it did," I said, pushing the boy out of my way.

The boy bent down and daubed his finger on my right
shoe, streaking it with black polish. "Good night, Mike!" he
shouted.

"Well, God damn you!" I said. I raised a hand to hit him
and he moved away, laughing.

"Don't hit him," said Charlie. "I tried it in Turkey, and
the punk pulled a knife on me."

The boy came back. He ran in front of me, bent down,
and spat on my shoe. "Good night, Mike!" While he was
bent over, I bumped him with my hip, and he lost his balance
and sat down on the pavement with a thud.

"Keep walking," said Charlie. "We could get knifed." We
kept going. When the boy didn't follow us, I looked back.
He was chasing a pair of middle-aged European women.

The man we had been sent to see was not an Arab. He
had been born in Egypt, although his ancestry was Lithuanian. He was a merchant, as were most of the Lithuanians in

Cairo, and he spoke excellent English, fluent French, flaw-less Arabic, and some Lithuanian. He used French in the conduct of his business, and so, he said, did almost all Egyptians of European descent. A dark, pudgy man, he had a broad grin that crinkled his eyes and made his glasses slide down his nose.

When we had introduced ourselves, he presented a friend of his to us, an Italian who had married an American girl and was working for the American Embassy while waiting for papers that would permit him to go to the United States.

We talked of our trip for a few minutes, and then the Lithuanian interrupted and said, "Do you take notes on your travels?"

"Yes," said Charlie.

"Please never put my name in your notes."

"All right. Any reason?"

"It is not a good idea. You will see why as we talk."

"He thinks everything is wired and censored and tapped," said the Italian. "He thinks there are spies for the government in the Hilton."

"You can laugh," said the Lithuanian. "You are going to America. You are already as good as a citizen. They can't touch you. With me, it is different."

The Italian shrugged his shoulders. "Enough," he said. "We should have lunch." He turned to Charlie and me. "Would you honor us by joining us for lunch?"

We thanked him and said we would be glad to.

"Wait a moment," said the Lithuanian. "I received a letter from your friend in Jordan. He asked me to do anything I could for you. Do you need anything now?"

"Not that I know of," said Charlie.

"Money?"

"We'll have to change some money sometime, but I think we're all right at the moment."

"When you change your money," said the Lithuanian, "change it with me. At a regular tourist bureau you get a bad exchange, what they call a tourist exchange. I will give you a realistic amount."

"But then how can you get the same amount for the travelers checks?" I said.

He smiled. "Now you will see why I don't want my name in your notes. For all the time you are in Egypt, you come to me and I will give you any money you need. You give me nothing. Then when you get back to America, you will be kind enough to deposit the dollars in a bank account for me. It is the only way I can get dollars, and the only way I can get any money at all out of the country."

"I don't mean to be nosy," said Charlie, "but why do you need to get money out of the country?"

"I will explain it all to you later," said the Lithuanian. "Now let us go eat."

We stood up and moved toward the door. "Oh, I forgot," said the Lithuanian. "You must swear never to mention my bank account to anyone. If you are going to talk about me, disguise me so no one will know who it is. The penalty for anyone caught with a bank account outside Egypt is life imprisonment."

At lunch, Charlie and I tried to talk about Egypt, but the Lithuanian refused. "Not here," he said.

"There you go again," said the Italian. "He thinks all the waiters are spies."

"You never know," said the Lithuanian. "Remember your friend. He didn't say very much, and look at him. No business."

"His business was going anyway. It was a fluke. Besides, it wasn't a waiter, it was the owner of the restaurant. They'd been friends for a long time. My friend thought he could trust him."

"A fine friend! Regardless, it never hurts to be cautious."

The second course arrived. It was chunks of lamb on a skewer, resting on a bed of saffron rice. "You know," said the Italian as he brushed a piece of rice off his shirt, "I am in a kind of dilemma. For one who is almost an American citizen, I have a badly unpatriotic attitude."

"How so?" I said.

"I'm not sure. I admire America and respect her, and even from this distance I suppose I love her, though I can't be certain. But America does so many things wrong."

"America makes mistakes, if that's what you mean. I don't see how that should make you unpatriotic. I don't know too many countries that never make mistakes."

"It's not mistakes. It's that I think I'm disappointed with America, even before I get there. I've been taught all the things she stands for, and all I ever see is hypocrisy. America seems to have a double standard almost as bad as Russia's. You say you believe in one thing, then you go and do something which contradicts it."

"Do you mean going back on our word?" said Charlie.

"No. It has nothing to do with promises," said the Italian. "It's in your whole policy. It's what you claim to believe. Look, you say you are against tyranny, right? You say you will not support any government that suppresses its people, that denies them freedom of choice, correct? You say you are fighting for democracy."

"Right," I said. "And look what we're fighting: Russia, China, Cuba—"

"Cuba! You're against Cuba now, in *this* time of oppression. What about the time before, with Batista? What did you do when he was in power? You maintained diplomatic relations and gave him aid. Near the end you realized he was on the way out, and your newspapers started writing articles against him, but that was all."

"Oh. Well—"

"Look at your allies. Not the neutrals, but your allies. In Europe alone, you have two allies that are unabashed dictators, Franco's regime and Salazar's. You wish to see some oppression? Go to Spain."

"I know about Franco, but do you know what would happen if we didn't support him? There'd be uprisings, because there would be no food, no supplies of anything. And the Communists would probably be in there in a flash. If they didn't support Franco himself, they'd have him overthrown by supporting all the rival groups. Then wouldn't that be nice, having a Communist country boxing in southern Europe?"

The Italian said, "So you think Communist oppression is, by its very nature, worse than Franco's oppression?"

"Yes. Communism will spread. Franco's regime at least has no designs on anything outside Spain."

"I will accept that, although it seems to indicate that you feel Spain can only have an extreme government, extreme right or extreme left. You preach democracy to these countries without believing it can work for them."

"But—"

"No, wait. I've thought about this before, and I've made a mental list of all the dictators you support. Some call themselves presidents, some kings. Spain and Portugal we've mentioned. Then there is the Shah of Iran. He is certainly not

as bad as some, but he does not by any means allow a representative government. In Pakistan you support Ayub, who
runs an unpopular, tight-fisted, tyrannical regime. Not only
do you support him, you arm him with jet fighters. And look
at the whole Middle East, run by a string of dictators who
accept your aid and then, with few exceptions, stash a lot of
it away in Switzerland for themselves. But you keep pouring
it in, even though the people are still as poor and all the
money's doing is larding up a few petty tyrants against the
day when they'll be overthrown. Of the neutrals, you support
Nasser, because you know if you don't he'll go directly to the
Communists."

"For God's sake, keep it down!" said the Lithuanian.

"Then there is Sukarno, the absurd little hysteric who
knows how to make both you and the Russians pay. You
don't want to lose Ghana, so you pour money into Nkruma's
dictatorship so some fool can buy himself a gold bed. On the
list so far we have six dictatorships, three kingdoms, and a
sheikdom. Shall I go on?"

"No. You've made your point."

"I'm not trying to be unreasonable," said the Italian, "and
I do see your point about certain dictatorships being prefer-
able to Communism. The unfortunate thing is the appearance your policy creates. Even if someone has never heard
Americans speak about making the world safe for democracy,
he must judge on what he sees. And what he sees is America
being very cautious, not daring to overthrow tyrannies, and
the Russians being progressive, revolutionary. They *do* overthrow governments, and the common man never hears of the
Russian brand of oppression. Our government won't print
it in the papers, and where it is printed, most of the people
can't read. All they hear is that such-and-such a government

—well, take Batista's, for example—has been overthrown and that that is good. Yet those that hate their own government, like the Spanish and the Jordanians, see the tyrants reinforced by planes and guns and boxes of supplies from America."

"Are you going to eat your food?" said the Lithuanian. "If you sit here and argue like this, someone will think something is strange. It is not wise."

"Oh, Lord," said the Italian. "He's off again."

We arranged to meet the two of them the next day. They had said they would take us on a sightseeing tour, to the pyramids, the bazaars, and the mosques. We thanked them for lunch, and walked to a museum next to the hotel.

"The Lithuanian may sound silly," said Charlie as we walked along, "and it's easy for the Italian to laugh. He's safe. But I think the Lithuanian is scared, really scared. I'd be interested to know just why he's so scared."

"Well, he said he's got that bank account."

"It's more than that," said Charlie. "I'm sure of it."

The next day, the Lithuanian and the Italian picked us up at the hotel and drove us to Giza. We stood for a few minutes at the fence enclosing the Sphinx, which has been made by photographs to appear three times its actual size, and we thought of climbing one of the pyramids, then decided against it when we stood at the base of one of them and saw how many steps it would take to get to the top.

Near the Sphinx were men who offered camel rides for fifty cents. A portly American woman paid one of the men and struggled aboard his camel as her friend stood to one side with a camera. The beast heaved itself to its feet, and the woman clutched the pommel of the saddle. When her friend had taken some pictures, she said, "Let me down now."

The camel's owner, who was holding the rope, smiled. "You give me dollar," he said.

"I've already paid you," said the woman. "Now let me down."

"You give me dollar," said the man.

"I will not," said the woman. "Get me off this beast!"

The man jerked the bridle, and the camel threw its head back, bouncing the woman in the saddle. She gave a short yelp and grasped the pommel tighter with both hands.

"Elizabeth!" she screamed. "Do something!"

Her friend strode over to the man, the ripple soles of her walking shoes crunching on the gravel. "Listen here," she said, "either you let her down this minute, or—"

"*You* give me dollar?" said the man.

"Most certainly not," she said. She raised the camera over her head. "I'll strike you with this camera if you don't let her down." She waved the camera by the strap.

The man laughed and jerked the bridle again. This time the camel reared slightly, barely lifting its two front feet off the ground.

"Elizabeth, give him the dollar!" screamed the woman in the saddle. "Give him anything, but get me off here!"

"I most certainly will not," said Elizabeth. "This is outrageous. I'll stand right here until the savage lets you down."

"*You* can stand right there, but *I'm* the one who's up here! Give the man his dollar."

"It is not *his* dollar. It's—"

The camel threw his head back. "Elizabeth, please!" screamed the woman.

"Oh, all right," said Elizabeth, reaching in her purse.

"But I think this is shocking." She held some coins out to the man. "I don't have an American dollar," she said. "Will you take piasters?"

The man took the coins and clucked to the camel, which dropped to its knees. The woman scrambled out of the saddle and slid down the camel's back. The man directed a mocking bow to them as they fled toward the tourist rest-house a hundred yards away.

"Why didn't you do something?" I said to the Lithuanian. "You speak Arabic."

"And get mobbed by all this filth?" He pointed to the groups of sleepy Arabs who were selling postcards and souvenirs by the Sphinx. "No, thank you very much."

We had a Coca-Cola at the resthouse, and then drove to the Mohammed Ali mosque, the massive memorial and place of worship that sits on a high hill overlooking all of Cairo. Below us the city shimmered in the hot sun, and the white and gold spires of the mosques dotted the landscape like jewels on a bed of velvet. In the distance, all the way across the city and the river, we could see Giza and the three tiny specks that were the pyramids.

"The city is beautiful," said the Lithuanian.

"It sure is," said Charlie.

The Lithuanian paused for a moment, then shook his head. "But it is also a great shame."

"What do you mean?" I asked.

"What is happening to Cairo. And to Egypt. It is a shame."

After he had looked around to make sure no one was listening, the Lithuanian began to talk about his life in Egypt. Ever since Nasser had begun his practice of nationalizing businesses in Egypt, all the small merchants had lived in fear and uncertainty. The government gave no warning. It decided, as if on a whim, that certain businesses would at a given moment become the property of the government, and a man who was making £300 ($650) a month from his own business suddenly found himself on the government payroll at perhaps £100 a month. The government avoided charges of thievery by "buying" the businesses with government bonds of twenty-year maturity, bonds that even the most patriotic Egyptians considered worthless.

"I will give you an example of the ruthlessness of this man Nasser," said the Lithuanian. "Always Egypt has had to import its wine. Many Egyptians love wine, but it is impossible to find a good grape that will grow in the desert. So one man, a foreigner, set out to develop that certain grape. He bought a small piece of dry soil and labored for twenty years on his grape, and he succeeded. He developed a grape that would grow well in the desert, and he began to make wine. It is a fine wine, and the first Egyptian wine we have had. Since there were no duties, he sold his wine cheaper than the imported wines, and he sold a great deal of it. He became a very rich man, but he did it by helping the country. He started a new industry, saved the people money, and provided many jobs. Even under Farouk he was only admired, never disturbed. But when Nasser came in, he took the man's business away from him. He said the man was making money from Egyptians, and no foreigner can do that. The man lost everything. Nasser gave him nothing for all his years of work, not even the houses and money he had accumulated for himself. Nasser took it all."

The Lithuanian's own business had not been nationalized —yet. But he had it on good authority that all businesses like his would be taken over within a year. He wasn't sure.

He knew the axe was hanging, but he didn't know for certain when it would fall. And once his business was gone, he was sure that he would have work for at most one year, until he could train someone else. He was a Christian, and Christians are not welcome in Egypt. When a Christian loses one job, he is prohibited by the government from getting another. It is part of Nasser's policy of "Egypt for the Egyptians," and to the Arabs, Egyptian is synonymous with Moslem. The policy was started when Nasser took the jobs away from all Europeans and forced them to leave the country. Europeans had given Egypt most of her industry and had developed her potential wealth. Their work was not, to be sure, totally unselfish, but it resulted in community profit, like the winemaker's efforts.

The Lithuanian was secretly planning to leave Egypt. The planning had to be done in secret because it was the only way he could hope to salvage any money or any belongings. The government would treat him exactly as it treated the Europeans—if he left, he would be allowed to take nothing but the clothes he wore, no foreign currency, no Egyptian pounds, no hard goods. Thus he had opened a bank account in the United States and was desperately trying to put money in it. And thus he was slowly smuggling his possessions out of Egypt. He had sent some jewelry with a friend to Jordan, some old gold coins with a friend to Canada, some precious Swiss francs, hidden for two years in the false bottom of a drawer, with a friend to France.

"Did you lose any of it?" said Charlie.

"I have no way of knowing," he said. "I am getting a visa to Canada, and from there I can get a visa to the United States. From here it is not a long wait to get into Canada. It takes more than ten years to obtain a resident visa in the

United States from Egypt. When I reach the United States, I will see how much of what I sent arrived. In my situation I must trust people. I suppose it is a good thing, trusting people. It is always safer to trust a friend with a job than to pay a stranger to do it. Of all my friends who have left Egypt, only one lost a lot, and he was the only one who actually paid a man to take large sums of money out with him. The man ran off with everything. I think an act of trust based on friendship is better than any business agreement."

"We'll take some stuff out for you," said Charlie.

"No," said the Lithuanian. "I wouldn't put that burden on you. I have some friends who are taking short trips abroad, and they will take it for me. They have done it before, and they know all the ways to do it safely. Also, they know the full extent of the risks they are taking."

"But that's just it," said Charlie. "With us, there would be no risk. Even if they caught me, they wouldn't do anything to us. I mean, nothing serious, anyway."

"They *could* do a great deal, but they probably wouldn't. They would fine you and perhaps detain you for a day or two, and they would make mention of the incident to your embassy. It is not worth it, either to you or to me, for if you do get caught, look what I lose. No, my friend, I thank you for the offer, but I cannot accept. The people I will send my valuables with are very experienced in this field."

"What would happen to you," I said, "if you were caught?"

"I'm not sure," said the Lithuanian. "I think about it often. For the bank account alone, I could be put in prison for the rest of my life. I imagine that would be my punishment."

"If they could get enough on him," said the Italian, "they might shoot him."

The Lithuanian turned and looked at him coldly. "I am aware of that," he said.

As we drove back into town, we passed through one of the new housing developments that have sprung up in Cairo's poorer sections. The buildings, six- and seven-story apartment houses, were built of concrete. They were new, but already cracks appeared in the walls. Broken windows were left broken, and jagged pieces of glass were all that was left in most of the frames. Tier upon tier of laundry hung drying between the buildings. It seemed that once having built these houses, the government had denied all responsibility for their upkeep and operation. They were left as a *fait accompli*, as if the government had wanted to prove to someone that it was doing something for the people. No one had told the people, who had spent their lives in mud huts and ramshackle lean-tos made from tin sheeting and cracked boards that they found in the street, how to live in a real house, how to keep clean, how to maintain a semblance of order. We got the impression that the people were simply picked up bodily and shoved into these houses, and that the whole package was immediately displayed to the world and then forgotten.

Women still washed their clothes in the street, and children lay in the gutter below the washing and sailed paper boats in the swirl of water that flowed down the street into the drain. A bus careened around a corner, full of workers coming home at the end of the day. It was so crowded that people hung from the window ledges and the chrome stripping when there was no more room inside. The bus stopped in the middle of the street, and the people poured out, yelling and laughing and pushing.

"These are the people that believe," said the Lithuanian. "These are the people who will follow Nasser through any

war, through any hell on earth, because they believe in him."
He blew his horn at the crowd, trying to make an opening
for the car. A few people shuffled lazily to one side, but the
crowd was still a solid wall in front of the car. They jeered
at the Lithuanian and shook their fists at him. He leaned
harder on the horn. A few more people moved, but the way
was still blocked. The jeering grew louder.

"They know their day is coming," said the Lithuanian,
"and they shout as if to say, 'wait and see, wait until it is our
turn.' "

Finally, the crowd broke, and the Lithuanian drove
through, still leaning on the horn. The high-pitched, jeering shouts followed us down the street.

"It's more difficult every day," said the Italian. "Today they
moved out of the way just a little slower than they did yesterday. Tomorrow they will move a little slower than today."

On the way back to the hotel, the Italian asked to be
dropped at the American Embassy. He said he wanted to go
over some business with his assistant. The Lithuanian did
not drive into the embassy driveway, nor did he park on the
street in front of the embassy, which was completely free of
cars. Instead, he approached the building from the rear and
left the Italian more than a block away from the entrance.
I asked him why he hadn't driven up to the door.

"I cannot afford to be seen too often around the American
Embassy," he said. "Someone might notice me there and
start talking."

"What's wrong with being with Americans?" asked Charlie.

"Nothing. Only it is not wise to make a habit of it. Someone might suspect something and start checking on me. Then
by accident it might become known that I am planning to
leave. I do not want that to happen."

*   *   *

The following afternoon we boarded a train which would take us up the Nile to Luxor and the Valley of the Kings. We allowed ourselves the luxury of berths for the overnight trip, and for thirteen hours we lay in the cramped compartment, digging sand and dust out of our ears and mouths, running our tongues over our gritty teeth trying to rid ourselves of the feeling that our mouths were full of chalk. We tried to seal the cracks around the window and door with pillows and raincoats, but the dust floated through anyway and settled in and on everything, even our eyelashes, so every time we blinked we dropped grains of the foul powder in our eyes. I awoke twice during the night, convinced that I was choking to death, and coughed and hacked over the edge of the berth until, exhausted, I fell back on the hard mattress and gasped myself to sleep.

The first day, we toured with a group from the hotel where we were staying. The monuments were magnificent, huge mausoleums carved out of the soft stone of the desert. Much of the decorative painting remains, and Charlie and I marveled at the bright, clear colors and the intricate details that had been laboriously set into the stone four thousand years ago. The entrances to most of the tombs are small openings that lead thirty or forty feet below the surface of the desert, for almost all the tombs are underground and show no trace of themselves aboveground. I wondered how anyone had found the tombs in this vast expanse of unmarked sand, and the guide said that they had been found as a result of some of the most fortunate thievery in history. Since the pharaohs were buried with their servants and with all the people who had worked on the tomb and who knew where it was, the only people who could locate the tomb after it had been sealed were the high priest and his followers. Very often, the high priest would wait a few years, then go back and loot the tomb of all the treasures of the pharaoh, not bothering to reseal it when he was through. Then he would blame the theft on some unsuspecting slave, have him murdered, and the case would be closed. Or if the high priest himself didn't loot the tomb, one of his descendants, to whom he had passed on the secret of the tomb's location, would sneak off into the desert and come back a rich man. Since they had first been opened, some of the tombs had been used for shelter by travelers and as temporary homes by nomads. Thus it is very rare, said the guide, to discover a tomb that has not been opened and looted, and thus museums treasure what little they have in the way of jewelry and tools and household goods of the pharaohs.

There were two Harvard professors on the tour with us, and as soon as we got back to the hotel, the elder, a thin, balding man in a gray suit, rushed to the bar and gulped a double scotch-on-the-rocks. He asked us to join him, and we sat down as he ordered another drink.

"Combats bilharzia," he said, lifting his glass. "Got to kill those worms." Bilharzia is a disease caused by parasites that inhabit the Nile, and it attacks many of the people who live on the river, slowly destroying their brains and eventually killing them. "Hang around that river all day, and the worms'll get you for sure," said the professor. "Barman! A scotch."

When the sun was low in the sky and the temperature had dropped well below a hundred, Charlie and I walked out along the river. It was the month of Ramadan, the Moslem equivalent of Lent, and from the towers of the mosques came the high, wailing call to prayer. The river was quiet, and flecked with red and gold from the setting sun. Small sailing boats, their sharply triangular sails barely able to fill in the light breeze, cut back and forth across the water. Robed Arabs paddled and poled their flatboats along the still shore. Women were washing clothes on the bank opposite, squeezing water through them and beating them on flat rocks. Thin, dark-skinned children dangled their feet over the sides of the ramshackle riverboats moored to slanting wooden posts sunk in the mud.

For the first time, I felt a deep sense of the exotic. To our left, up the river, was the Sudan, and after that, Uganda and Kenya and Lake Victoria and Tanganyika, names redolent of romance and storybook excitement. It mattered not at all that the romance and excitement most probably did not exist. Sitting under a palm tree, watching the sun sink beyond the desert and hearing the melodious cry from the mosque as it drifted across the water, I could have found glamour in the name Newark.

I was awakened at six o'clock Wednesday morning by the sound of beating wings. I rolled over and wiped the sweat from my eyes and forehead, sat up in bed, and found myself staring face to face with what I was sure was the biggest kite in the world. The bird, a relative of the hawk, was perched on the edge of the balcony outside our window, and he was gazing at me over his hooked beak with his big, round, dark eyes. I waved an arm at him, to show him that I wasn't dead and wouldn't make a tender breakfast, but he simply shifted his feet under his hefty body and craned his neck forward.

For no reason at all, it occurred to me that today was the 14th of February, Valentine's Day. I leaned across to Charlie's bed and thumped him on the shoulder. "Hey," I said. "Wake up. Someone's brought us a present."

Charlie lifted his head off the pillow and said, "Huh?"

"Someone brought us a present."

"For what?"

"For Valentine's Day, of course. Look." I pointed to the bird, who had jumped to the window sill and sat with his head cocked curiously to one side.

Charlie pushed himself into a sitting position and opened one eye. For a count of three, the one eye stayed half closed. Then suddenly both eyes popped open with an almost audible click as the thin lines of sleep were torn loose. "Omigod! A vulture!" The bird sat bolt upright, as if denying an unpleasant epithet. Slowly, Charlie reached behind him for his pillow. When he had the pillow firmly in his grasp, he flung his arm around and fired the pillow at the bird. "Duck!" he cried, diving under the covers. The pillow went wide and struck the side of the window. The bird watched it fall to the floor, then pecked at a mite under a wing. He blinked once at Charlie, once at me, and turned casually away and jumped off the windowsill, flapping his wings.

We hired our own guide for that day. He was a man of at least seventy, tall and gaunt with a thick nose and a shaved head. Despite the heat, he wore a long black overcoat. We rode in horse-drawn carts to the ferry that shuttles people back and forth across the Nile. We could see the souvenir sellers on the opposite shore, already gathering by the cars that take tourists to and from the Valley of the Kings and the Valley of the Queens.

Along the road, people slept in the shade of their mud huts, or sat with their backs to the dusty walls and covered their faces with their robes. Flies clustered on the sleeping people, drinking from the corners of their eyes and the sides of their mouths. Even those people who were awake didn't bother to brush away the flies, and when we stopped for a moment by the side of the road, we saw a mother with a nursing child permit flies to gather around the nipple and the sucking mouth and drink from the moisture. One fly drank at the outboard corner of each of the baby's eyes, and flies drank from the mother's eyes and pendulous lower lip. I turned to the guide, who was sitting next to me, and said, "Why don't they brush the flies away?"

"It is useless," he said. "They always come back. We have long since stopped brushing them away." He turned full face to me, and I saw a large black fly sitting at the corner of his left eye. We drove on. "It is not bad," said the guide. "The flies only drink. They do not bite." A few yards farther on, we passed a little girl who was selling oranges at a stand made from an empty crate. The flies, bold and persistent, clustered around the oranges, and the girl held her hands over her face and shook her shoulders. "Only for such as she are they bad," said the guide. "She has not yet learned to accept them. As she grows older, she will learn." The flies rested on every orange and on practically every inch of uncovered flesh on the girl. From time to time she shook her head violently and stamped her foot.

A fly landed on my hand, and as I slapped at it, it made no attempt to fly away. It rolled dead to the floor of the cart. "They're spoiled," I said. "They have it too easy."

We spent the morning looking at carvings on the walls of the temples. There were the stories of the lives of the pharaohs and their queens, of wars and conquests, of gods and miracles. At one point, the guide lowered his raspy voice and whispered to us that he was going to show us something he had not been able to show for months, because there had always been ladies on his tours. This was something for men only. He took us to a remote corner of a large temple and showed us the story of the god of fertility, a strapping lad with endowments that could only have been a myth. Carved on another wall was the Egyptian version of the Annunciation and the Virgin Birth. The sun god, whose local name was Ammon, came to a woman and told her that she was to have the honor of bearing a child by him, and that the child would be the ruler of the two Egypts, upper and lower. Thus was born the first of the line of pharaohs, who were to the Egyptians the direct descendants of God, as Christ is to the Christians the son of God.

We stopped at a resthouse, a hastily built structure of loose planking and tin sheets that sat in the open desert between two underground tombs. We had been willing to wait for food until we got back to the hotel, since resthouse food in Egypt is notably dull and often bad, but the guide said he would appreciate it if we would take shelter from the sun for a few minutes. Charlie and I ordered Cokes, and we offered one to the old man. He shook his head.

"Then can I get you a glass of water?" said Charlie.

The guide ran his tongue over his parched lips and spat dryly onto the sand. "I cannot," he said, "but I thank you."

"You can't?"

"Not until the evening meal," said the guide. "In the month of Ramadan, we cannot eat or drink until the evening meal. We cannot even swallow our own spittle." The edges of his lips were coated with white foam where his spittle had dried.

"No water?" said Charlie.

"Nothing," said the guide. "That is why I asked you to rest here for a few moments. For a man of my age it is hard to fast all day in the desert without weakening." He paused and spat again. "But I will not keep you here long. Just a few moments."

"Not on your life," said Charlie. "We'll stay here as long

as you want, till *you* feel like moving. We're in no hurry."
The old man smiled and said, "You are kind."

We drank our Cokes in silence, enjoying the tingling coolness of the liquid as it wet our mouths, but swallowing
quickly to avoid the sticky-sweet aftertaste that Coke leaves
when it gets warm. When he had returned his empty bottle,
Charlie said to the guide, "Do you approve of Nasser?"

The question took the guide by surprise. "Why, of course,"
he said. "He is a great man."

"And what about Farouk?"

"A bad boy, Farouk. A silly, stupid man. He should not
have had a place of such importance. He was more concerned
with women and drink than with his country. His self-
indulgence paid him slight reward in the end."

Charlie said, "Why is Nasser such a great man?"

"You need only look to see the great things he has done,"
said the guide. "I am told that in Cairo he has built wonderful new houses for the people. There is evidence of his great-
ness even here. You have seen the roads that lead from the
river to the monuments. They are fine roads, you will agree."

We nodded, remembering the narrow, roughly tarred
roads.

"Those roads used to be all dust and dirt. A year ago,
when the King of Morocco came to Egypt, Nasser ordered
the roads improved, and within a month they were tarred!
It has made life a great deal easier for us."

"Would he have ordered the roads tarred if the King of
Morocco hadn't come?" said Charlie.

The old man looked at Charlie, then turned and spat into
the sand. "Would you?" he said, and he leaned forward on
the table and pushed himself up from his chair. "It is time
to go."

At the end of the day, the guide took us to some souvenir

shops. Most of the shops sold junk, he said, but he would show us where there was good ivory. Charlie bought two or three ivory letter openers, and I bought an ivory cigarette holder. The next day, a jewelry dealer in Cairo told us that our "ivory" was polished buffalo bone.

9

At SEVEN O'CLOCK Saturday morning, we boarded a Middle East Airlines Viscount for Jerusalem, Jordan. The night before, we had dined with the Lithuanian and the Italian and their wives at a floating restaurant called Omar Khayyám, a lavishly decorated barge on the Nile. We settled our accounts with the Lithuanian, who gave us the name of his bank and the number of his account. We each owed him about ninety dollars. As we parted, he said, "I will see you again. Next time, in America."

The plane had to fly a circular route, over the deserts of Egypt and northern Saudi Arabia and Jordan, to avoid violating Israeli air space. We flew low, and the ride was bumpy because of the currents of hot air rising from the desert. We saw no towns, no roads, and no people during the flight, only the dry, red desert and the empty shoreline of the northern end of the Red Sea.

It had been ninety when we left Cairo early in the morning. When we landed in Jerusalem, it was forty-four.

As a result of the Arab-Israeli conflict, Jerusalem is a divided city—half lies in Israel, the other half in Jordan. Ironically, the birthplace of Christ, the Garden of Gethsemane, the Way of the Cross, and Calvary are all on the Jordanian side, in the Old City. It seemed to us strange that we should have to go to an Arab country to find the seat of Christian tradition.

Charlie had passed through Jordan when I was in Rome, and he had met the head of a small tourist agency who had found him a cheap, clean hotel. Charlie called him from the airport, and he drove out and picked us up and took us to another cheap, clean hotel.

The man was a stocky, olive-skinned Arab with a thick mustache, who wore American suits and had studied English in Chicago. During the next few days, we spent a great deal of time with him, because we were dealing with him about a complicated, only half legal way for us to purchase a multi-stop airline ticket through to New Delhi. At one point, when his negotiations nearly broke down, I confessed to him that I had long harbored a secret wish to drive across the Iranian and Afghan deserts to India. But as soon as I mentioned this to the man, he put a stop to my fantasy by saying, "Great idea! I'll arrange everything. Let's see, you'll need one Land Rover, a tent, provisions, a guide, two or three automatic rifles and two or three pistols—in case you run into one of the many bandit gangs—one or two thousand rounds of ammunition, a spare for every part of the engine, four extra tires, and innumerable gallons of gasoline. I'll get it all for you. The only thing I can't get for you is the course in how to completely dismantle an automobile engine. But somebody around here will know where to send you. As for price . . ."

Charlie leaned over and gave me a fatherly pat on the shoulder. "Brilliant thinking," he said. "I'll meet you there."

When business was slow, the man and/or his helper guided us around the old city. One afternoon we were driving through the hills outside of town, and the man said, "By the way, I never asked you how you liked Egypt."

"It was fascinating," said Charlie. "But now we're trying to figure out which word fits Nasser better, tyrant or malevolent dictator."

"What do you mean?"

We told him of the oppression we had seen, the snatching of businesses and the prejudice against and treatment of Europeans, and we described the lack of progress and the police state atmosphere. We said that Nasser was violating a tenet that we, as Americans, considered inviolable: the right of every man to use his talents and his sweat to improve his lot, the principle of free enterprise. His attacks on the individual were, we felt, tyrannical. We added that we felt the only conceivable argument in favor of tyranny was that it is efficient, and Nasser's regime was hardly efficient. It had not as yet managed to justify its oppressive nature by sufficient concrete improvement.

Though the man was reluctant to talk about his own government, since he didn't know us well and felt that loose talk about his government was unwise, he spoke openly of Nasser. He began by attributing our lack of understanding of the problem to the differences between the Oriental and

Occidental minds, which made Charlie and me impatient. It seemed that he was going to explain away everything in abstract terms, and the nationalizing of people's businesses was not, to us, abstract. He also said that the Oriental mind was so completely alien to Westerners that we might never understand it. But his point was more concrete than we thought, and as he explained, we saw that he was not hedging at all.

The Oriental mind and temperament are, he said, governed largely by emotion, almost never by reason—especially when they have not been guided by education. It is a dangerous mind, for once it has been seized by emotion, there is little that can change its course. Its mass instincts are very strong, and a mob led by a convincing orator with a cause, good or bad, is often unstoppable. Most of the people in Egypt are uneducated, and until the time when they can receive sufficient education, they must be held in by a tight rein. When Nasser came to power, he shouted about injustice. He is a good speaker, and he fired the people with words about tyrants, oppressors, and imperialism, and told them that he was their savior and would give them all that Farouk and his predecessors had withheld. He gave them some food as a token of his good faith and promised to effect miraculous changes in their lives.

Once they had had even the slightest taste of a better life, there was no stopping them. They saw that the way to get food and clothes and the riches that had never been theirs was simply to take them, for that was what Nasser himself was doing. Moreover, they had a cause. They were fighting injustice, Nasser told them so, and it was very convenient to have the fight against injustice benefit them. Whereas they had always been docile, accepting their fate and never challenging their masters, suddenly they saw that they could challenge, and that challenging brought results.

To save Egypt from chaos, our guide went on, Nasser had to put the clamps on. He regulated the press, to keep the fanatics out of print, and he outlawed gatherings that might incite a crowd to thievery and murder—all in the name of his own fight against injustice. But even as he enforced his iron rule, he knew that he had no time to waste. The people would not sit idly by and wait for gradual reforms. They were through with being grateful and had become demanding instead. He had to move fast, had to enact his reforms as quickly as possible, and the only way to get the money to do that was to nationalize all profitable businesses. He needed every piaster he could get, and he did not have time to buy up businesses gradually. Besides, if he simply took businesses, he would receive more money than if he bought them and waited for them to show a profit. Ninety-five per cent of Egypt's wealth lay in the hands of five per cent of the people. Nasser himself had told the ninety-five per cent of the people that this was the case. He had to get at the wealth before the mobs did. His method would ruin five per cent of the people, but there was every reason to believe that it would give Egypt new life and, eventually, do a great deal of good for the people as a whole. It was, in a sense, a half-democracy: it believed in doing what is best for the majority, but it neglected the other side of the coin, individual freedom.

The guide admitted that Nasser still had nothing impressive to show the people for all his nationalizing. And, he added, the people were getting restless. But Nasser did have some proof of his good works: he could show the people that their former masters, the "oppressors," no longer had the wealth and could not hold power over them. He was driving all the Europeans out, creating an "Egypt for the Egyptians." It was their country, and soon they would be reaping the great fruits of their years of rewardless labor. The state had the wealth, and the state, said Nasser, was the people.

But when his reforms begin to take effect, said the guide, when he can redistribute the land and build good houses and start the long process of educating the people, he will relax his controls. He must hold the people down only so long as he has nothing concrete to show for all his talk, for the people do not realize that it takes time to create a whole new government and social system for a country. They want to be shown right now.

Although the guide's explanation did not lighten the repugnance Charlie and I felt for any policy of thievery cloaked in terms like "nationalizing," and although neither of us could recall any dictatorship that had voluntarily evolved into a democracy, it did leave us with a very uncomfortable doubt. Is it possible that a certain end, if it is broad enough and worthwhile enough, can justify *any* means? *Can* you let ninety-five per cent of the citizens of a country live in abject poverty because it is wrong to take property from a man without paying for it? *Can* individual freedoms be held in highest importance when a country is trying to cleanse itself of the filth spread over it by a recently deposed dictator? In the United States, we have never lived under a dictator. Wealth has never been as unequally distributed as it was in Egypt—or, for that matter, as it was in czarist Russia. In the United States, the government can safeguard individual freedoms without condoning the oppression of anyone. Can we judge all peoples by our own standards?

The guide took us to see the birthplace of Christ. It was raining, and a cold wind blew the rain almost horizontally over the hills, so it stung our faces as we ran across the courtyard in front of the shrine. "Despite the weather, you are here at a good time," said the guide when we were inside. "In another month, you wouldn't be able to move in the streets. People come from all over the world to spend Easter here."

The "inn" is now a small room in a church. The floor is of rough stone, and around the walls are altars and candles and displays belonging to nearly every Christian sect. "No one is sure exactly where in this room Christ was born," said the guide, "so every religion picks a spot and tells its followers to worship that spot as the actual one. The Catholics are over there, the Greeks there, and different Protestant groups are all around the room."

The guide's helper was a young Jordanian student who was working to put himself through school. He was about our age, and because he had few opportunities to talk to Americans other than those middle-aged ladies and retired gentlemen whom he escorted during the Easter season, he was eager to spend time with us. He walked us through the old city and along the Way of the Cross, and every ten minutes or so he asked if we would like to stop for a cup of tea and "a little chat." By the end of the day, we were bloated with fifteen or twenty cups of the tepid, milky tea. Though we couldn't know it then, our tea-drinking bouts with him were good training for our forthcoming socializing with tea-crazy Indians.

The young man had the same fear of the police and of informers as the Lithuanian in Egypt. He always took us to dark, quiet restaurants and sat in the shadows in the back of the room. He told us it was safe to assume that one out of three Jordanians over the age of eighteen was in the police, the secret police, or in some respect on the government payroll as an informer. He was violently anti-Israel, but not, as is common, violently pro-Arab. He was more concerned with affairs in his own country than with any pan-Arab movement. And his anti-Israel feeling was more personal than political. His family owned a farm in Palestine and had been forced to flee during the terrible years of chaos and massacre after World War II. Though the farm was still standing, and though he maintained a fierce, driving desire to reclaim his land, he had no real hope of ever seeing it again.

The more we talked to him, the more I was impressed with his intelligence, his alertness, and his broad range of knowledge. He could talk intelligently and thoughtfully about France and Algeria, about Russia, about America, about India and Pakistan and Malaya, while the best we could do was trip lightly over the surface of most of these countries. And his knowledge was not only political: he had read Molière, Dostoevsky, Hemingway, and Confucius, had studied Tocqueville's *Democracy In America,* and was an ardent devotee of dixieland jazz. I was sure that a lot of his education had been acquired secretly, and the difficulties he had overcome to get this education made his knowledge even more impressive. His desire to learn, to know, to understand, must have been great indeed, but at the same time I felt that his life must have been sadly lacking in the idle pleasures and silly amusements and leisurely, hedonistic joys that we had known in school and college.

Had the young man been unique in our experience, he would not have bothered us. We would have been able to

consider him extraordinary and let it go at that. But as we
met more and more students in the Middle and Far East,
we saw that his drive and his knowledge, though strange to
us, were the rule rather than the exception among students.
Charlie and I talked often about the difference between
students in the East and students in America, and we tried
to fathom what it was that gave students from Egypt to
Japan this burning, single-minded drive toward knowledge.
Or, on the other hand, what it was that made American
students (and, to a certain extent, all students in the West)
comparatively so lethargic and disinterested. When we were
in college, most of our friends knew something about
politics, and most read a paper every day, or at least glanced
at the headlines on their way to the sports section. But very
few had a deep interest in the nation's affairs, to say nothing
of the world's, and still fewer had an all-consuming cause
or even a strong belief. Half the students in most colleges
couldn't locate Burma on a map and couldn't tell you the
name of the King of Jordan. More than half had no idea
of the arguments on either side of the India-Pakistan dispute.
The attitude of American students has traditionally been a
sort of *Je m'en fou* attitude—it doesn't concern me, and
the hell with it.

It was not until we had talked to students all over the
world that we were able to discern any reasons at all why
foreign students were so much more alert than those in
America.

The difference between the West and the rest of the
world is partly a difference between old and new. It is not,
as the Russians would have the world believe, a difference
between decadence and vitality. Although China and
Japan and India had civilizations which were thriving when

people in the West were still wearing blue paint, of all the systems of government in the world today, the West's are the oldest. America's dates from 1783, Russia's from 1917. England's is three hundred years old, Communist China's is fifteen. France's is about to have its ninety-fourth birthday, Egypt's has yet to have its twelfth.

When our government was created, there were no exact precedents and few established ideas or methods or beliefs. There was a national purpose, the establishment of a good, viable system of government, and all men were challenged to carry out that purpose. Everything was new, everything was exciting, and in everything there was a sense of discovery and achievement.

Today, our government and the other governments of the West are secure in their traditions. Our beliefs are no longer new and exciting; they are cherished and respected. Our government has worked well for almost two hundred years. Nothing has shaken it, no one has effectively challenged it. As much as people may argue with certain acts or administrative policies, they will seldom question or try to alter the basic system of government. Certain people may try to reinterpret the freedoms and rights of Americans, as in the segregation question, but that is as far as anyone will go.

So American students do not feel they must search for and get excited by new ideas. They know their traditional beliefs are right for them and for their country, and they have no quarrel with them. Until recently, there has never appeared a serious threat to these beliefs, and they have had no cause for worry. They feel that a successful past is a guarantee of a successful future. What does it matter to them if the Imam of Yemen is overthrown? Such changes have never affected them before, and they find no reason to assume that they will now. Who cares who the president of Pakistan is, as long as he doesn't try to interfere in our lives?

The people in the Middle and Far East are where we were a hundred and fifty years ago. Nothing is secure for them. They accept nothing and challenge everything. They are being wooed by democracy and by Communism, and they live in fear that one system or the other is going to be forced on them by America or by Russia. Everything that happens to their neighbors concerns them. A Pakistani student is concerned about the independence of India. If India goes communistic, his country has no bulwark against the Chinese. And he must know what is going on in America, for from America come all his arms and much of his food.

So as paradoxical as it may be, perhaps America has been at a disadvantage in being the strongest, most secure country. We have never been challenged, and thus we have never been made to think. We could afford that lack of thought when the realities of the world permitted us to follow a policy of complete isolationism, but when the realities changed, when it became imperative for us to enter into competition with the rest of the world, it suddenly became very costly.

The situation is changing for the better, though what is forcing the change is for the worse. As our beliefs, our way of life, even our lives, have been threatened more actively each year, as our security has slipped away, it has become apparent that we *are* affected by what happens in other countries, that we *must* be informed about what goes on in the world. A boy who has never known what his rights and

aims and principles as an American are learns suddenly,
when they are challenged by other principles and other aims,
by Russians or Germans or Cubans. Everything he has
blindly taken for granted abruptly takes on new meaning for
him.

Even since 1961 there has been a significant change among
college students. There are far fewer now who disavow all
responsibility and conscience by shouting, "Better Red than
dead." The various college political clubs have made national news more than once by articulating their intelligent,
well-founded views. Student newspapers and magazines that
used to deal in their editorials with purely parochial matters
have adopted a broader scope and are voicing thoughtful
and informed opinions on world affairs. And perhaps most
significant, every year fewer young people support the same
political candidates their fathers support. They are learning,
instead, to think for themselves.

There is only one way for foreigners to go from Jerusalem,
Jordan, to Jerusalem, Israel—on foot. Charlie and I were
checked out on the Jordanian side of the Mandelbaum Gate,
and carrying fifty to sixty pounds of luggage apiece, we
trudged through the tortuous maze of sandbag barricades
and concrete tank traps that divide the two countries. On
the Israel side of the border, the customs official offered to
give us special pieces of paper for the admission stamp so
that we could return, if we wished, to an Arab country. No
tourist can enter an Arab country if he has an Israeli stamp
in his passport. Charlie accepted the special stamp, I did
not, for no better reason than that I wanted an Israeli stamp
in my passport and had no intention of returning to an Arab
country. It began to snow as we waited for a taxi to take us
to the Jerusalem YMCA.

Israeli Jerusalem is a dull city. There is little to see—all the religious and historical sites are on the Jordanian side— and little to do. There were no live theaters, and no night-clubs, and we knew no one in the city. We had dinner at the only big hotel and then took a bus to a movie theater on the outskirts of town which was showing *Please Don't Eat the Daisies* with Hebrew subtitles. The impression we got was not of a city made drab by poverty—indeed, compared to Cairo and Jerusalem, Jordan, this Jerusalem was thriving. The main street was lined with shops selling European clothes, sporting goods, and furniture, the houses were clean and in good repair, and the people were well dressed and seemingly prosperous. Rather, it seemed to be a city populated by businessmen and students who had no interests outside their occupations, who cared little, if any, for entertainment, and who plodded along from day to day, traveling only from home to work and back again, asleep by ten-thirty and awake by seven. Jerusalem seemed to be a city in name only.

Tel Aviv is a city. We took the train down through the hills to the sea. The land, though rocky and inhospitable, was all being worked—either for olive trees or, wherever possible, for crops. A few miles from the city, as the train started down from the crest of a long hill, we saw the icy blue of the winter Mediterranean curving along the shore below sparkling white buildings as high as ten stories.

People were everywhere in the streets—gathered in groups on the steps of municipal buildings and museums, sitting at tables in porched-in cafés, hurrying to and fro along tree-lined avenues. There were ads for theaters, movies, and concerts on every street corner, newsstands selling everything from the *New York Herald Tribune* and the London *Times* to *Paris Match, Life,* and *Whisper.* The

women were as well dressed as Parisiennes, clicking along
the streets in pointed-toe shoes. They wore light spring
dresses, either not knowing or not caring that the temperature was barely forty.

We had planned to stay in Israel about a week, hoping to
go to Haifa and the Sea of Galilee. But we found that we
would have to leave in less than two days. Although our
Jordanian guide had managed to arrange for an open ticket
to New Delhi routed through Teheran and Karachi, so
that theoretically we could go as we pleased, he hadn't been
able to obtain a schedule of planes flying out of Israel, and
it turned out that we had arrived at a spectacularly inop-
portune time. Either we left Israel the next day or we
stayed for ten more, when the next plane stopped on its
way to Teheran. By going to Cyprus and one or two other
places, we could have routed ourselves through Baghdad on
three different airlines, but we had already been informed
that we couldn't go to Baghdad: first, we had no Iraqi
visa and couldn't get one in Israel, and second, we would
lose our typewriters at the border—the premier, Abdul
Kassem, was having trouble with the Kurds, and he was not
willing to allow any potentially useful items such as typewriters into Iraq and perhaps into the hands of reporters
sympathetic to the rebels.

So we spent only one night in Tel Aviv. A woman named
Virginia Hall, a foreign service officer I had met in Rome,
invited us to dinner, and we spent the evening steeped in
Israeli culture—drinking scotch and listening to records of
that famous Israeli cantor Ella Fitzgerald singing the plain-
tive oriental melodies of Cole Porter.

10

I HAD put out of my mind the trouble Bob Resky and I had had finding a hotel room on the Riviera, and I was developing a rather cavalier attitude toward the problem of finding a place to sleep. Charlie and I had reserved our room in Egypt more than a month in advance, and in Jordan and Israel we either met or already knew people who found us our "cheap, clean hotel." We were becoming spoiled, sure that in any city something would turn up. We were aware that the room would, on occasion, have to be in the best hotel in the city and therefore cost ten to twenty dollars a day, and would other times necessitate our walking the dark, unfamiliar streets at midnight and settling for a filthy, sometimes dangerous, fleabag lean-to for forty cents a day. In Europe or America such fleabags were relatively safe, and though we had heard that to stay in a twopenny-hapenny dump on the docks of Singapore was to invite disaster, we couldn't conceive of a disaster ever occurring.

We had not reserved a room in Teheran. The girl at the BOAC office in Tel Aviv advised us to reserve through her, but we hoped to get a cheaper room by looking around ourselves. As the plane circled around Lebanon, sedulously avoiding Arab air space, and soared over the twinkling lights of Ankara into the night, I wondered if we had been wise in refusing to let BOAC reserve for us.

At thirty-three thousand feet I have to talk. It is the only pastime that keeps my mind off the fact that through some insidious feat of legerdemain, I have been catapulted into the sky in the belly of a creature that has no right ever to leave the ground. If I'm forced to sit and contemplate this unpleasant fact, I can convince myself that within no more than thirty seconds the flying mass of metal will plummet back to the earth it never should have left in the first place.

I had had two quick drinks as soon as the seat belt sign went off, and already the sweat that had soaked my palms during takeoff was drying and the lump that almost closed my windpipe when the engines changed pitch at crusing altitude had all but disappeared. I turned to Charlie to discuss the hotel situation, but he was dozing, infuriatingly unperturbed by being at the mercy of this devil machine. The plane was not crowded, and so when the stewardess brought me a third drink, I asked if she knew of any hotel in Teheran that would fill our needs. She was almost six feet, slim, with a pleasant figure and a head of curly blond hair. She spoke with a clipped London accent.

"I don't know if I can help you," she said. "There's always the place we stay, but the rooms are a little dear. Are you there on business?"

"No," I said. "Just touring."

"It's a terrible place, Teheran. You shan't want to stay long."

"What's wrong with it?"

"Not a bl . . . not a thing to do, is all."

"And what do *you* do there?"

"We get the whole crew together and have our own parties. We stocked up on gin in Jerusalem. You certainly can't go *out* anywhere. The only thing worth seeing is the market, unless you like belly dancers and that rot." She sat on the arm of the seat across from me. "Of course, sometimes we get that at our own parties, if the crew's lively enough. This is a good crew."

I said, "Do you think there'd be any rooms in that hotel for us?"

She laughed. "I'll ask about. Meet me in the terminal when we land, and I'll tell you then." She walked down the aisle to answer a call from a woman who wanted an extra pillow.

The hotel was named the New Naderi, and it was, as the stewardess had said, expensive. But we arrived late at night, and we were unwilling to walk the streets with no idea of where we were going and no recommended hotels to look for. The desk clerk called two slightly cheaper hotels, but both were full. Besides, by now we had met the whole crew, and they had invited us to a party as soon as we unpacked. We resigned ourselves to the expense and, after throwing our bags in our room, rushed downstairs and drank warm gin-and-limes with the crew until 2 A.M.

First thing in the morning, Charlie called a man on his list of Eisenhower Fellows from Teheran. The man was out of town, skiing. The second man on the list was out of town, too, as were the third, the fourth, and the fifth. Charlie contacted the sixth man, who had a position in Iranian industry, and he asked us to lunch that day.

Our first stop was the American Embassy. We talked to one of the political officers, and he asked us what we knew about the country. Charlie said that all we knew was what we had read in the papers, and that the papers had led us to believe that things weren't as rosy as they might be. We gathered that the Iranian government was not riding the crest of success just then. The senate and parliament had not met for weeks, having been adjourned indefinitely by order of Prime Minister Amini. And the university had recently been closed because of violent student riots. The riots were over a minor matter of personnel changes and had nothing to do with complaints against basic governmental policies or procedures, but many people feared that Communists would infiltrate the rioting mobs and fire them up to overthrow the shah. For all we knew, we had arrived just in time to see a leftist revolt.

The man pooh-poohed our alarm. He told us that the government was running very smoothly. Indeed, he said, it was running better than normal, because the shah's recent redistribution of land had been very popular, and he was going to continue to give land to the peasants for years to come. The political situation, in other words, was stable. True, there were problems, like foreign exchange deficits, student riots, lack of education among the people, but Amini was a strong man and was handling the government well, and there was no reason to fear for the shah or the shah's regime. We were given some booklets on the agricultural and industrial situations in Iran and we went on our way, assured that everything was normal and that the country would prove to be of no interest to us if we were hoping to see an Eastern state in turmoil.

But before Charlie had left America, he had been told again and again to search for facts not through an embassy staff but through the people of the country. Diplomats, after all, do not live the life of the natives. They are governed by different laws, they see different people, and many of them almost never see the natives. So when we lunched with the Iranian businessman, Charlie skipped the routine questions about ways of life, standards of living, and the national growth, and asked the man bluntly what he thought of the shah and the shah's reforms, of the student riots, of the closing of both government bodies, and of the whole political situation in Iran. Had the man not chosen to trust us, the rest of the lunch might have been spent in uneasy silence. But he recognized our lack of authority with the government and our honest curiosity, and spoke freely. Charlie told him what the man at the embassy had said, and he laughed.

"I wonder where he gets his information," he replied. He added that he wanted to make it clear, first of all, that he was living in a tightly run police state. Second, it was obviously to the government's advantage to have people think everything was stable, and therefore anything the government said about its stability was to be regarded with suspicion. He pointed out that things could not have been just fine if Amini had found it necessary to suspend all parliamentary activities and all higher education. The very existence of a police state showed a basic instability. It was all very well, he said, to claim that the police state was necessary, but its necessity derived from the strength, or the potential strength, of the opposition. Why bother to stamp out public opinions if there are no opinions that can hurt you?

According to our new friend, Amini's position was not

at all safe, for the leftist groups were gaining strength by settling their differences. But as happens when people fight against an absolute rule, their policies were negative rather than positive, bent upon ousting the shah and not supported by constructive plans for a government thereafter. So if they did manage to join forces and take over, there would first be chaos because of the lack of any clear policy, then another tight rule when and if order came. The man was not certain that there would be any government whatsoever by May. As it turned out, the shah survived and Amini did not. He resigned, a frustrated and disappointed man.

But even though he did survive, the shah's position was not comfortably secure, and to this day there are many people disenchanted with him. The landowners, who are among the few educated, capable people in the country, are naturally unhappy seeing their land turned over to the peasants. The leftists remain equally discontent.

We are still wondering about what we heard from the man in the American Embassy. The easiest explanation, and the one that is probably true, is that he saw no reason to talk to us about the weakness of the shah's government. He had no way of knowing that we wouldn't go shouting it about. He didn't know that with our connections and authority, we could have shouted it from the rooftops of Teheran, Moscow and Washington and no one would have listened to a word.

But perhaps that wasn't the case. Suppose he had been telling us what he really thought about the situation. He talked to us for almost an hour, and he didn't hesitate to tell us the problems Iran was having with border defenses or with Russian threats, or with farming or bad bureaucracy or American aid. I would far rather believe that he was simply unwilling to talk freely to us, that he was holding out.

We did not see the Iranian businessman again. The day after we had lunch with him, he went south to Shiraz on business. And since we had exhausted our "educational" contacts, we spent the next three days with the BOAC crew. We toured the covered bazaar with our blond stewardess, who drew a crowd like one Jayne Mansfield would draw in Times Square. Well over six feet in heels, her blond hair shining in the sun, to Iranians she was a strange and wonderful sight, a golden goddess of love walking in their midst.

The crew warned us against Karachi. "A pesthole," they said. "Not a bloody nightclub in the whole place. And *hot!* The only thing to do is stay at the airline resthouse and live in the swimming pool. That way, you'll meet some people, and you'll have a party or two. Otherwise, you might as well skip through to Hong Kong. You won't find any laughs in *this* part of the world.''

When we left Teheran late one evening, the temperature was forty-five, so we were pleased when the stewardess on the PIA jet announced that in Karachi it was eighty-eight. It didn't occur to us that at one o'clock in the morning, a temperature of eighty-eight degrees did not indicate a very temperate climate. And as we descended the ramp from the air-conditioned plane, all our joy at being warm once again quickly disappeared. Karachi's eighty-eight was like no eighty-eight I had ever experienced. The Egyptian climate had been hot, but it was dry, and after the initial cascade of sweat as our pores opened, we had gotten used to it. In Karachi it was like being in a bathtub. A breeze from the sea nearby did not waft across the land; it flowed. Everything was wet—the runways, the walls of the buildings, the metal railings in the customs office. I asked a customs official when the rain had stopped.

"Six months ago, sahib," he said. "It will begin again in twelve or fourteen weeks. But is it not lovely, sahib? When the moon is out, everything glistens in the wet air."

By the time we were through customs, our coats, jackets, and ties were draped over our suitcases. My pants stuck to my legs and made my underwear ride up my thighs.

At the airline terminal in downtown Karachi, we were told that there was a hotel only three blocks down the road, and since there were no cabs, we would have to walk. We gathered our clothes and our suitcases and struggled down the unlighted road. It was a wide road, bordered on one side by flat land leading to the sea, on the other by dense tropical growth—banyan trees, heavy, rubbery plants ten feet tall, and gnarled, sinuous vines that wound their way between the huge leaves of the plants and trees. And the growth was alive. Birds and monkeys cheeped and cawed and barked among the trees. They were like city noises—traffic that honks and beeps endlessly, eventually becoming a soothing undertone. Silence along that road would have been terrifying.

The night clerk in the hotel was a filthy, surly little man who seemed to take pleasure at the sight of us, weary and sweating. He didn't understand a word we said. After a few minutes of trying everything from French to rudimentary deaf-mute sign language, we raised our voices, somehow thinking that would make him understand, and the racket woke one of the clerk's superiors, who stumbled out of a side room, fidgeting with his necktie and brushing his hair out of his eyes. He snapped at the clerk in English, not Urdu, and suddenly the clerk's English came back to him. "May I help you?" he said, with a wicked smile.

The heat, the vegetation, and the animal sounds from the

jungle were all new to us, as we had expected them to be, but it was the hotel that first made us realize we were in the East. So far, the hotels we had stayed in had in no way reflected the culture or history of their various countries. They were cheap, clean, unimaginative and sterile. The Nile Hilton was something else again, but still not Egyptian by any stretch of the imagination. But the Hotel Palace in Karachi reeked of tradition. It was undoubtedly one of the oldest hotels in Pakistan, and its days of glory must have been during the British raj. The rooms were large and high-ceilinged. Two monstrous fans twirled slowly above the beds, discreetly supplemented by a small air-conditioner that hummed behind a curtain. A sign informed us that we could not keep our bearers in the room with us, but that the hotel would be delighted to accommodate them in their servants' quarters.

After we settled in, a room boy, roused from his nap on the cool tile floor of the hall, shuffled into the room, bowed, set two thermos bottles of ice water on the low table in the living area, bowed again, and mumbled, "That is all?" He passed through the thin double doors and closed them behind him. We double-locked the doors, tested the locks, and found that with a hard pull they sprang open. We slid a bolt across the top of the doors, tested them again, and they held, though loosely. As we pondered various hiding places for our passports, a piece of white paper slid under the door. It was the standard hotel document disclaiming responsibility for lost or stolen articles. We found a desk drawer that could not be pried open from the back or from the underneath, fitted our own steel lock to it, deposited our passports and travelers checks, and went to bed. A friend in New York had told me that in India and Pakistan it was advisable to put all valuables in the bottom of one's pillowcase and sleep on them.

I put a switchblade knife there instead, and during the night it woke me four times by sliding down the pillowcase and rapping me in the head as I rolled over.

In the morning, Charlie got out his list of Pakistani Eisenhower Fellows and began calling. Not only did he reach the second man he tried, but the man invited us to the beach the following day.

As we walked through the lobby, we were stopped by a dark young man in a white shirt and black slacks, who asked us in clear, unaccented English if we could use his services as a guide. We had decided to use no more guides: we had needed the old man in Egypt to explain the temples to us, and the man in Jordan to drive us around. But guides were expensive, and after a tourist agency bus tour of a city we were usually well enough oriented so that we could find our own way around. We depended on guidebooks and on friendly strangers who would give us directions. We told the man this. He smiled a condescending, you-have-a-lot-to-learn smile and said, "In Pakistan, your method will be of no use. There is no agency tour of Karachi."

"Then we'll roam around on our own," said Charlie.

"I would advise most strongly against that," said the man.

"Why?"

"You would have a miserable time. You do not speak our language, so you could not ask directions. You cannot buy a guidebook, so you wouldn't know what to look for. You dare not tell a taxi driver to take you somewhere, for he will take you all around the city trying to avoid the place you want. That way he can run up the bill. That is, if he understands you in the first place. If you find your way to the market, you will be set upon by beggars. The crowd is so thick that you can't move about easily, and so you can't escape them. If you are rough with them, you will find yourselves surrounded by an angry mob who may do nothing or who may rob and beat you. If you give something to one of them, others will push and shove to get near you and will point their stumped arms or their leprous feet at you. It will be a nightmare."

We asked how much he charged, and he said we could get his services and all cab transportation for six dollars per half day. We very quickly agreed.

He was an excellent guide. He took us to Victoria Park, to the seashore, to the center of the city, and to the market, where he showed us that his warnings had been well-founded. Filthy, sick people in tatters jammed together and pushed and elbowed and called out prices for their goods. Cows lay in the streets, sleepily confident that no one would disturb them. Flies covered everything—the food, the people, and the cows, spreading dung among the bags of spices. Old men sat on the sides of the streets with their hands outstretched, groaning and rolling their eyes as we passed. A young boy whose legs had never grown but had rather twisted into gnarled stumps pushed himself along on a dolly and turned over on his back to raise a begging hand to us. Bands of children chased us through the streets, screaming shrilly, and pushed us and grabbed at our shirttails until the guide drove them away with an angry threat. They retreated for a moment, then came back, only to be shoved away again.

The guide's name was Robbie. He had been born in Karachi, and because his father had had some money, he had been able to go to school. But his father did not have a lot of money, so he was unable to get the education required for a career in business. He had decided to be a guide because it was the most profitable career open to him. In the tourist season, he worked five or six days a week, which, when he deducted his expenses, netted him twenty-five or thirty dollars a week, a good living in Pakistan. He had two children, both girls, and because they were girls, he did not have to send them to school. He himself could teach them whatever they ought to know. If he got the time, he said, he might teach them to read. It wouldn't matter much to them either way, since their lives would be focused only on their households. His hobby was trying to perfect his English; he learned three or four new words each day.

Robbie wanted to impress on us that he was not a typical Pakistani. He wanted to disassociate himself from his countrymen, to be thought of as a man with a sophisticated Western mind. He showed us letters he had received from satisfied customers and told us of the many interesting conversations he had had with an American zoologist on a trip they took into the wild northern country of Pakistan. He would say, "You have heard of Utica, New York?"

"Yes."

"Then perhaps you know Mr. Arnold Gardner. I have here a letter from him. I will show you."

"I'm afraid we don't know Mr. Gardner."

"Well, let me see. I have a letter from Mr. James Bergman, of New York City, New York. Sixth Avenue. Do you know Mr. Bergman?"

When Robbie found that we did not know Mr. Bergman, or Mr. Fisher or Dr. Molloy or Dr. Williams or any of his other American clients, I think his opinion of us fell. This did not, however, prevent him from asking us to write a letter for him.

We went to a mosque in the center of the city. It was a huge pink building, surrounded by terraces and pools and footbaths. Hundreds of Moslems wandered about the courtyard, and hundreds more knelt inside the mosque, which was designed to accommodate four thousand worshipers at once. Robbie was critical of the amount of ritual in Islam.

"It is unrealistic," he said. "I am a Christian, and I believe in God, but I do not go through all the bowing and scraping. I go to church every Sunday, and that is all. This chanting and lying down and praying five times a day is a pagan habit, don't you think?"

Charlie, who is a Roman Catholic, said he thought it was all right if the people wanted to do it, and that they shouldn't be criticized for performing their religious obligations.

"You are right," said Robbie, "but it is pagan nevertheless. Pakistanis are like that. They believe in a lot of ritual. It is not a very sophisticated religion, Islam. It is not modern."

"Modern!" said Charlie. "What religion is modern? Judaism is old, Catholicism is old, Buddhism is old, all—"

"Yes, but certain kinds of Protestantism are new. I am a Unitarian, and that is modern. That is a religion of today."

"Now what do—" Charlie stopped. A very dark woman dressed in a ragged black robe was tugging at his sleeve and rolling her eyes. Charlie started to say something to her when suddenly he noticed that she had a baby strapped to her back. The baby was white—not albino, just Caucasian white—and it had long blond hair and Western features. It looked like a refugee from a New Canaan nursery. "Is that hers?" asked Charlie.

"Yes," replied Robbie. He said something to the woman, and she spat on the ground at his feet. She walked away.

"That's *her* baby?"

"Yes, and she is an outcast because of it. It is a shame that in this day and age society still excludes people for such an unfortunate thing. It is not her fault."

"But how can that be her baby?" I said. "I mean, even

if she had married a white man, the baby would be darker than that. That baby is pure Caucasian."

"No, it is the result of a terrible thing. You would think that medical science would have found a cure for it by now."

"What terrible thing?"

"When the woman was pregnant, poor soul, she drank milk after eating fish. It was inevitable. The baby had to come out like that."

"I beg your pardon?"

"Yes. It is a sad sickness. The woman knew it would happen, but she was weak. And modern society shuns her for being weak. It is a shame."

"Are you serious? You believe that?"

"Of course. It is a known fact. Ask anyone what happens if a pregnant woman drinks milk after eating fish. The child will come out white. It is horrible. I would rather not talk about it." Robbie turned away and started toward another part of the mosque.

I stood there for a moment, still not sure that Robbie was serious. But he was, and he had been almost angry when I prodded him.

Charlie nudged me forward. "Welcome," he said, "to the mysterious East."

The Pakistani Eisenhower Fellow picked us up at our hotel at ten o'clock the next morning. He was in his early thirties, with fine, strong features and eyes so dark that I could not tell where the iris ended and the pupil began. His black hair was brushed straight back. "Good day," he said as he got out of his car. "My name is Pyarali. Did you know that Arthur Miller has remarried?"

On the way to the beach, he said, "One of my favorite

pastimes is arguing, so I hope you won't take offense at anything I say. If I seem curt or snappish, it is nothing personal."

"Understood," I said.

"Good. I mentioned that only because I was thinking of
saying something, and I did not want you to think me rude."

"What was it you were going to say?"

"I think your Vice-President Johnson is a very stupid
man." He added, "Perhaps not always stupid, but he was
stupid when he was here."

"How so?" said Charlie.

"He was stupid when he asked the camel driver, Bashir
Ahmed, to come to America. You remember that?"

"What was wrong with that?"

"I will grant you that he was only trying to be generous,"
said Pyarali, "but he did not stop to think. The poor people
in Pakistan are not proud of being poor and illiterate. They
are ashamed of it, and they feel your Mr. Johnson was being
very condescending to Bashir Ahmed, that he was ridiculing
him for his poverty and ignorance."

Charlie said, "How the hell do they get *that* idea?"

"He was taken to your country and shown around, and he
said he had a wonderful time. Our people think he was
being taken as an exhibit, a freak, a poor, stupid man from
a backward country. He had never heard of all your appli-
ances, and your papers carried amused accounts of his surprise and fascination at something as basic as a flush toilet
or a washing machine. Mr. Johnson meant well, I'm sure,
but he kept saying, 'Do you want to come to *my* country?'
as if he wished to show us how life really is. It was showing
off. My people do not like to be made to feel any smaller
than they are. They resent the manner of your Mr. Johnson."

"Not *all* Pakistanis feel that way, do they?" asked Charlie.

"What is bad is that it was he who did it. If it had been one of your congressmen, it would not have created such a bad impression. People are used to them and expect them to act like bums."

"Congressmen?" I said.

"Yes. I think they are your greatest liability abroad. It is not your tourists, who have an exaggerated reputation. It is your congressmen. From all I can gather, two-thirds of the educated people in the world think all your congressmen are bums and thieves. Look. It is this sort of incident." He stopped the car and looked through his wallet until he found a newspaper clipping. He handed it to me and started the car.

The clipping, from the foreign edition of the *New York Herald Tribune*, was about a congressman from one of the Middle Atlantic states who had just returned from a trip abroad. He had filed his expense account, and it indicated an expenditure of $115 per day. Of that amount, $50 was listed as "miscellaneous." When he was asked about that category, the congressman replied, "Oh, you know, cabs and tips and things." The other $65, he explained, paid for his hotel room and his meals. Dinner each night cost $20. He said he had had many obligations to discharge. He had had to take people to dinner every night.

When he had read the clipping, Charlie said, "Okay, it's bad, and it does happen. But I don't think you can generalize from one thing like this and say all congressmen are bums."

"You would like more?" said Pyarali. "How about your Southern Democrat congressman, the one that got so drunk before his arrival in Spain that he had to be given oxygen on the plane and helped off by two aides. They wanted to leave him on the plane until he sobered up, but there was a welcoming committee there to meet him. He said he was ill. I'm sure he was! I would be, after a bottle of whisky.

"And about your counterpart funds. We keep money on deposit for your officials, as you do for ours, but not so they can stuff their own pockets. A group of congressmen came over here on an around-the-world 'inspection tour' of something or other, and they practically bought out all the good stores. They bought jewels, silks, gold, everything. There is the 'miscellaneous.' And these are the people who run the United States of America! These are the men the people of the United States elect to office. It does not endear me to the American people when these men come here and are loud, offensive, bossy, smoking their cigars and spending money, not even *their* money, like water. When they leave, they say in their parting speeches how much they have learned about the people of Pakistan. The only time they ever see the people is from the windows of their cars as they drive to and from the airport.

"I know what the problems are," continued Pyarali. "They are twofold. First, there are no moral qualifications at all for becoming a member of the governing body of the United States. In fact, a man needs very few qualifications, period."

"What does he have to be?" I said.

"You have to have been a citizen of the United States for seven years, must be a resident of the state from which you're elected, and must be twenty-five years of age. The second problem is that the only people who can change the rules, who can stop the spending and can tighten the qualifications for election to Congress, are the members of Congress themselves. Most of them were elected to support parochial causes, like cotton prices or the prevention of birth control, and don't know or care much about anything else. And they are not going to deprive themselves of anything, much less of the privileges they have granted themselves in Congress."

Pyarali turned the car onto a dirt road leading to the beach. "Finished," he said. "I am sorry to make such a long speech. But I ask you, I ask the United States, to do yourselves one favor: if you are going to elect these men, please keep them to yourselves, don't send them to us. You expend such great efforts to win the approval of the other countries of the world, and then you destroy all your good work by sending these awful men to check up on it. It is political suicide!"

Charlie and I heard the same speech time and again thereafter, from people all over the world. A few months after we had returned to the United States, I received a letter from a man we had met in India. It was a short note attached to a newspaper clipping. The note said, "An American friend passing through Delhi left a newspaper at our house. It was the NYHT, 20 September of this year. I enclose a piece of it." The clipping was datelined Boston.

LEGISLATOR—IN JAIL—NOMINATED

Former State Rep. Charles Ianello, who won renomination to his seat from his cell in Boston's Deer Island jail, hinted yesterday he may try for higher public office.

At a press conference in the jail, Ianello, 54, said he had a higher office in mind, but would not disclose his plans except to say it was not a state-wide office.

He was renominated for his seat in the Massachusetts House in the Democratic primary. In Boston's 8th ward, the Democratic nomination is tantamount to election.

Ianello is serving a one-year sentence for theft of $983 in state funds. A contracting firm controlled by his family was paid for sidewalk work that was never done.

On the bottom of the clipping, the man had written, "Is *this* the Democracy you're trying to make the world safe for?"

Pyarali had a small beach house on the shore of the Arabian Sea. There were other such weekend retreats to the left and right, some prefabricated, some fashioned of canvas and wood, and one of aluminum. A man walked a camel by the house and indicated that we could ride it for two rupees. Remembering the woman in Giza, we declined.

We swam and then had lunch on the porch. During lunch, I saw a man walking along the beach with a bear and a dog. I asked Pyarali what the man was selling. "I will show you," he said. "It is a pretty sight." He clapped his hands twice, and the man led the bear and the dog to the house. There was a short exchange between Pyarali and the man, and Pyarali gave him two or three rupees. The dog lay down in the sand. The man pulled the string that led to a brass ring in the bear's nose, and the bear stood on his hind legs. The bear's teeth and claws had been removed, and his slobbering mouth looked ridiculous with nothing but pink gums and flapping jowls. The man began to sing a high, nasal song, and he hit the bear lightly on top of the head in rhythm to his tune. Each time he tapped the bear's head, he pulled on the string, which made the bear jump and grunt. It was supposed to appear that the bear was dancing.

After perhaps five minutes, the man stopped the song and let go of the string. The bear dropped onto all four legs and then lay down in the sand, panting. The man turned and smiled at us and raised his stick with the kind of flourish with which a magician precedes a particularly impressive trick. He bent over and jabbed the dog just below the tail. The dog leapt to his feet and began to chase his tail, growling ferociously. He ran in circles, growling and snapping at himself, until the man tapped him with the stick. Exhausted, he sank to the sand.

Evidently the money Pyarali had given the man was enough to cover the super deluxe special show, for the man kept repeating his act. After the third repetition, I said, "Okay, I've seen it. Grand." Pyarali told the man he could go away now. The man stopped the act, but he did not go away. He began to gesture wildly and argue with Pyarali. Finally, Pyarali barked a command at him, and he dragged his animals off down the beach. "What was all that about?" I asked.

"First he wanted us to hire him to do the whole act again," said Pyarali. "Then he wanted us to hire him to pose for your cameras. Then he said he wouldn't go away unless I gave him some money. I told him he was welcome to stay there and do his act all day but I was not going to give him any more. It was when he started to curse me that I got so military and ordered him away."

We talked mostly about politics. Pyarali wanted to go into politics in Pakistan, but he was waiting until the government changed before he ran for office. In the Ayub government, most candidates are hand-picked by the Ayub cadre. Even if he could get elected to parliament, he would be a member of a puppet body, whose main *raison d'être* was to act as a display, a symbol of a democracy that didn't exist, and a front for the autocracy of Ayub. During a lull in the conversation, Pyarali said to me, "Let me see your hand." I held out my hand, palm up. "When were you born?" he asked. I told him. "You were born within an hour of midnight."

"Yes. I was born at about eleven-thirty at night. How did you know that?"

"The combination of the Taurus influence and this hand made it certain." He added something about an ascending moon that I didn't understand. He went on to give me a standard palm-reading. I asked him how much he actually believed in astrology. "Completely," he said. "It is almost a religion with me. I will tell you a story."

Since Pyarali was so interested in astrology, he had been studying it seriously for many years. He had visited a great many of the most renowned astrologers in Pakistan and India. Some were quacks, he said, and in fact the reputations of most of them were wildly out of proportion to their talents. However, three per cent or so were excellent, and Pyarali felt it was worth sifting through the quacks to get to these men. Three or four years ago, he heard of a man in Ceylon who was supposed to be the best. In his possession were thousands of rolls of dried leaves, and on each roll was written the life—past, present, and future—of one person. The rolls were called "life books." A friend of Pyarali's had gone to Ceylon to ask the man if he had his life book —the life books were not only of Ceylonese people, but of people from all over the world, and the odds were slim that the man would have his. But he did have it, and for two days Pyarali's friend sat and listened to the exact details of his past, present, and future. The fee for such a complete reading was enormous, but it was the reading to end all readings, and well worth the price.

Pyarali's friend told some of his friends about the man, and a few of them went to Ceylon to see him, but he did not have their life books. Someone had them somewhere, but it could have been a man anywhere from Tokyo to Cairo. One year Pyarali took his vacation in Ceylon, and he went to see the man. The man said he would look for Pyarali's life book and would tell him the next day whether he had it. He did, and that day he began the reading.

The writing on the leaves was in Tamil, and as the man read, his assistant provided a simultaneous translation into Singhalese, and Pyarali himself translated into Urdu. The reading began with the past of his present life, then went to his past lives, then to the future of his present life, and finally to his fate after this life. He was told his entire ancestry, complete with names, occupations, places of birth, ages at death, and number of children, all accurate to the finest detail. He was told his mother's age, appearance and past, and his father's age, appearance, past, profession, and achievements. He was told the place, year, month, day, and hour of his birth, the extent of his education, his profession, his illnesses, his ambitions, the number and sexes of his children, his wife's name and what she looked like. He was told what he wanted to do and that he would succeed to such-and-such an extent if he went about it in a certain way. Then he was told of his past lives. He seemed to have worked his way up the class scale in other lives, for his four or five most recent ones had been as either a prince, an adviser to a king, or the king himself. As for the future of this life, he was told how many children he would have, when and how serious their illnesses would be, and the exact steps toward his goal of being a prominent leader in Pakistan. He was told what to avoid and when to avoid it, how to cope with certain situations that were destined to arise, and what people to trust and distrust. And he was told at what age he would die, sixty-three. The man did not tell him how he would die. He would be lucky enough to have very few, if any, future lives.

In the whole reading, there was only one fact with which Pyarali disagreed: the life book said that his mother was one of seven children, and he knew that he had only four uncles and aunts. When he returned from Ceylon, he asked his mother about her family. She told him that her mother had lost two children in childbirth. She had not known it herself until recently, and she had not mentioned it to anyone.

We saw Pyarali every day until we left Pakistan, and we argued incessantly. Often he made statements exactly the opposite of his beliefs, just for the sake of argument. But one thing he felt very strongly was that the United States was paying too much attention to the neutral countries and not enough to her allies. Pakistan, for instance, was a solid ally of the United States. But this alignment with the West did no more, and possibly less, for the standard of living of the Pakistanis than India's policy of nonalignment did for the Indians. Pakistan is a tiny country burdened with the world's fifth largest population. Naturally, many Pakistanis looked at India, at the aid she received from *both* camps, East and West, and logically concluded that Pakistan's faltering economy could be much improved by neutrality. She would receive more than twice the amount of outside help, and she would be protected by everybody, so a large part of her defense budget could go to food and housing and education. "Also," said Pyarali, "what do you suppose a Pakistani thinks when he sees our great ally, the United States, pouring aid into India, a country with which we are practically at war over Kashmir? How long do you think we will stand quietly by as our so-called friend feeds our enemy?"

A year later, during the Chinese invasion of India, the

government of Pakistan, annoyed by our sending military aid
to India, opened negotiations with China about a nonagres-
sion pact and the construction of a road that would give
China easy access into India.

11

Because of a combination of confused circumstances, Charlie was unable to get an Indian visa before we arrived in India. In most countries, the incident would have been handled matter-of-factly: Charlie would have been (1) detained at the airport until a visa could be issued, (2) issued a temporary visa, or (3) sent back to the country he had just left. In India, the oversight almost caused a national disaster. The customs officials at the airport had no facilities for issuing visas and no facilities for detaining people for more than an hour or two. And there were no planes returning to Pakistan that day. They didn't know what to do, and what began as a simple colloquy between Charlie and one calm official ended in a shouting match between both of us and five muddled, furious Indians. Finally, after more

than a full hour's arguing, the Indians gave up and issued
Charlie a special, temporary, twenty-four hour permit and
told him to be at the immigration office the first thing the
next morning.

We took an airport bus to New Delhi and started looking
for a hotel. It was after dark when we found one that would
have us. It was a government hotel, cheap and clean, and
a room and a bath and three meals cost six dollars a day. We
ate a light supper, put our dirty shoes outside the door to be
polished, and went to bed.

At six the next morning, I was deep in a dream of my lost
lady love when the phone rang. I fumbled the receiver off
the hook and grunted into the mouthpiece.

"Room 406?" said a chipper voice.

"No," I said, "this isn't room 406."

"It isn't?" said the voice. "What room is it?"

"616."

"Are you sure it isn't room 406?"

"Of course I'm sure! I know my own room number. It's
room 616. And it's also six o'clock in the morning."

"Oh." *Click.*

I slammed down the phone and rolled over, hoping to
recapture the vision of loveliness. But it was gone, and I
buried my head in the pillow and waited for my mind to
find new pastimes.

The doorbell rang.

"What?" I yelled into the pillow.

"I'll get it," said Charlie. He stumbled out of bed and
undid the locks. The room boy stood in the doorway, crisp
and clean in his white uniform. "Yes?"

"When you wan' tea?" said the room boy.

"What?"

"When you wan' tea?"

"When do we want tea?"

"Yes."

"I don't know when we want tea. Who wants tea, anyway? Hey," he shouted over to me, "do you want tea?"

"Go away," I said.

He turned back to the boy. "What are you, nuts? It's not even six-thirty in the morning. We don't want tea. Who ever told you we wanted tea?"

"You wan' bananas with tea?"

"Now listen here, son. I don't want tea, and I don't want bananas, and I don't want cookies. And what's more, I don't want to see you again. Goodbye." He started to shut the door, but the boy put his foot in the way.

"You frien' he wan' tea?"

"No! Out! Hear? Out!"

We got up at nine-thirty. Breakfast was served until ten, so we shaved and dressed leisurely. At quarter to ten I opened the door to pick up our shoes. No shoes. I rang for the room boy.

"Where are our shoes?" I said when he arrived.

"I gedem," he said, shaking his head in a broad, vacant grin.

"Thank you."

He scurried off down the hall. In a moment, he returned with our shoes. I gave Charlie his. I was about to shut the door when I noticed white spots all over my shoes.

"Just a minute," I said. "What are these?"

The room boy looked. "Had mud onem," he said.

"Yes, they had mud on them. Why didn't you take it off before you polished the shoes?"

"No good."

"No good. You mean it came off his shoes but not off mine?"

"Yes."

"How do you suggest I get these white blobs off my shoes? They're hardened right in there."

"Give me money," he said. "I takem down to shoeman. He fixem." He stood there with that same grin on his face.

"Forget it," I said. "Just forget it."

I put on my shoes and we went down to breakfast. The menu said that we could have cereal, eggs any style, bacon, toast, marmalade, honey, juice, milk, and coffee. We did. The juice and cereal came, and we had those without incident. Then came the eggs. Charlie had ordered scrambled, I had ordered fried. Both orders were scrambled.

"I wouldn't try to change them if I were you," said Charlie. "You'll only confuse the waiter."

I ate them.

"Could I have some more butter?" said Charlie.

"And may I have my coffee now, please?" I said.

The waiter, a short, stocky man with heavy, dark eyebrows and a large mustache, grunted. He walked away. We finished our eggs and drank our milk.

"Where's our waiter?" said Charlie.

"I don't know." I looked around the room and saw the waiter standing at a serving table by the kitchen door. "He's over there."

"What's he doing?"

"Nothing." I motioned to the waiter, but he didn't see me. The captain came over.

"May I help you?" he said.

"Yes, please. We asked for some butter and coffee, and the order seems to have gotten lost."

"I'll tell your waiter."

"Thank you."

Five minutes went by. "Where's the waiter?" said Charlie.

"Same place."

"What's he doing?"

"Same thing. Nothing." I motioned to him again, and he saw me and came over.

I said, "What happened to the butter and coffee?"

"I gedding it."

"Where?" said Charlie. "In Singapore?"

The waiter grunted and walked away.

Five more minutes passed. "Where's the waiter?" said Charlie.

"Same place."

"Yeah, I know, and doing the same thing. Nothing. The hell with this." He raised his hand, and the waiter came over. "Do you think you could find the time to get us some butter and a little coffee?"

"I gedding it," said the waiter. He turned around, walked to a serving table not ten feet away, reached into a cabinet, pulled out a pot of coffee and a plate of butter, and brought them to the table. He set the pot of coffee down so hard that it splashed on the tablecloth.

"Thanks," said Charlie.

The waiter walked away.

After breakfast, we got the address of the immigration office from the hall porter. It was only a few blocks away, on the same road as the hotel, so we decided to walk. The number of the building was 44. We passed 38, 40, and 42. There was a large space between buildings, a wooded area in which sat four or five small houses, and then number 46. A sign on the gate before the wooded place said, "No admittance. For authorized personnel only. Barracks."

"It must be in there," said Charlie, pointing to the sign.

"It can't be. That says it's barracks. Besides, it says keep out. Maybe the number was 144."

"Let's ask." A man was passing by, and Charlie went up to him. "Pardon me," he said. "Do you know where the immigration office is?"

The man stared at Charlie. Then suddenly he grinned and began to move his head from side to side. It was a strange motion, a turning of the head which kept the chin almost stationary and moved the rest of the face left and right with the chin as a pivot point. This motion, combined with the broad, toothy grin, made the man look like an imbecile. "Gheegheegheee hahahahaha yes," he said.

Charlie was unnerved by the laughter, and said, "Oh."

The man gave no indication that he was going to say anything further, so Charlie said, "Is it here, or at number 144?"

"Gheeghee haha yes."

"Which?"

"Gheeghee haha yes."

"Is it far or near?"

"Hahahahaha yes."

"Oh. Well, thanks a lot anyway. Sorry to bother you."

"Hahahahaha yes." The man walked away, smiling.

"Try again," I said.

A man approached us. "You like see some pretty stones?" he said.

"No, thank you," said Charlie. "But perhaps you could tell me where the immigration office is?"

"You wan' pretty stones?"

"No, thank you. Would you tell me where the immigration office is?"

"You give me one rupee."

"No, I won't give you one rupee." Charlie turned away, and we started looking for someone else to ask when the man said, "Dad way." He pointed down the road.

"Down there? Number 144?"

"Dad way."

"Is it far or near?"

"Yes."

"Okay. Thank you." We started walking.

Number 144 was a tailor shop. We went in. "This isn't the immigration office, is it?" said Charlie.

The tailor was an old man, dressed in a tattered, western-style suit with a necktie somehow fastened to the side of his shirt collar. "No," he said. "It is not. The immigration office is number 44. It is like a forest with a few small houses. Pay no attention to the signs."

"Thank you," I said. "I'm afraid we have a language problem. We've been misguided. Sorry to bother you."

"Not at all."

"Language problem, nothing," said Charlie when we were outside. "That other guy was just getting back at us for not buying pretty stones. He'd have had us walk to Calcutta."

At the immigration office, we were told to wait. We sat down on a bench in a hall. Forty minutes later, a man came out and asked what we wanted. We told him we were trying to get a visa.

He laughed. "Oh, bad luck," he said. "You've come to the wrong place. Other immigration office. The one in Old Delhi."

"But the man at the desk said for us to wait here."

"I know. He didn't do it on purpose, he was just confused. Thought he might as well tell you to wait as anything else. Here's the address in Old Delhi."

In half an hour, after riding across New and Old Delhi in a Vespa taxi, we were seated in the immigration office in Old Delhi. There were eight men in the office, all at desks lined up against the wall. There were papers everywhere—on the floor, in bookcases, on the desks, sticking out of ledgers. Piles of papers completely obscured one man from the shoulders down. He sat behind them, meticulously entering numbers in different ledgers which he pulled down from a shelf over his head.

A man took Charlie's passport and temporary visa as soon as we arrived, and told us to have a seat. Charlie filled out a visa request form and presented two pictures of himself. The man went to a desk, took a large stamp from a box, and stamped the passport. "Your visa," he said, showing it to Charlie. Charlie reached for it. "Oh, no," said the man. "It has to be signed."

Twenty minutes later, Charlie inquired about his passport. "It is being signed," said the man. "The deputy has signed it. Now it is with his assistant. When he finishes, it will go to the chief immigration officer. Be patient, sir. It will not take much time."

Fifteen minutes later, Charlie asked again. "I will check for you, sir," said the man. He went into another office, and came back in five minutes. "The chief officer has signed it, and now it is being checked by the deputy and his assistant. They will initial it, and it will come back here to me." He sat down and began copying names into a book.

When another half hour had passed, Charlie got up to ask the man again. Just then, an office boy came through the door and handed the passport to the man. "One moment, sir," said the man. "I will just check it over once, and you may have your visa and go." He set the passport on the

edge of his desk and went back to his book. He copied two
more names, then sat back and lit a cigarette. He leaned
back in his chair and stared at the ceiling.

"Will you please check my passport?" said Charlie.

"I am doing it, sir," said the man.

"Oh, so I see."

The man came forward in his chair and smiled at Charlie.
"It is hot today, don't you think?"

"Yes, I do think," said Charlie. "And I would like to get
out of this office."

"Ah, yes, so would I. But it is not *too* hot this time of
year. It sometimes is much hotter. Especially in the hot
season. This is not the hot season."

"You don't say."

"Truly. The hot season will begin in, let me see, about
two more months. You should see it then."

"I hadn't planned on it," said Charlie, "but at this rate
I imagine I'll be sitting right here all through the hot
season."

"That is all one can do in the heat: sit. But this heat is
not so bad. It sometimes is much hotter."

"So you said. Look, could you please—"

"Your passport. I shall do it immediately. It is simply
that one must not rush in this heat. Things must be taken
slowly. It is very unhealthy to rush about in the heat." The
man took Charlie's passport off the edge of the desk and
set it in front of him. He opened it and went through it
page by page, looking at all the stamps and visas and exit
permits, and commenting from time to time on a particularly
handsome stamp or a permit in a strange language. When
he came to the Indian visa, he bent down over it and studied
it in minute detail. "What a shame," he said.

"Oh, good God," said Charlie. What's wrong?"

"The deputy made a mistake. He signed his name in the wrong place. I shall have to send it back to him." He stood up and started to walk out of the room, but the look of pain on Charlie's face must have touched him, for he stopped and returned to his desk. "Wait," he said. "I may be able to fix it myself."

"I sure would appreciate that," said Charlie.

"You realize, of course, that such a thing is completely out of the ordinary."

"Of course."

"I could get in trouble for this."

"I understand," said Charlie, "and I appreciate what you're doing for me."

The man took a stamp from the box and placed it on the visa so that the signature line fell right below the deputy's signature. "There," he said. "No one could tell." He stood up, and with a courtly flourish, handed Charlie his passport. "Here you are, sir, and I hope your stay in India is a pleasant one."

"Thank you for everything," said Charlie, and we left.

After two days of dealing with Indians, Charlie and I were on the verge of madness. Our tempers were short, and we snapped unreasonably at everyone, including each other. Then gradually we began to accept it, and we calmed down. We decided to find out what it was that numbed everyone and everything in India and imbued the whole society with a "who gives a damn?" lazy lack of concern. We had an appointment with a man who was arranging passes for us to an audience with Prime Minister Nehru, and we asked him about it.

"Some of the fault is ours, I can't deny it," said the man. "But a lot of it is Britain's. I'll explain it as best I can."

First, he said, the "Yes, sir, I'm doing it" and then never doing anything attitude is an extreme illustration of the apathy that a quasi-socialist government can produce. The Indian government gives practically no incentive at all to more or better work. Technically, a man can advance, both in position and salary. But most government employees realize that they are limited either by lack of education or by the size and confusion of the bureaucracy itself. Their jobs, filling out ledgers, stamping papers, or filing reports are simple, dull jobs that are either done or not done—no one can stamp a paper better than anyone else. It is very easy to be perfect in their work, impossible to be outstanding. So why should they work hard? They are given a job and told that this is what they are fit for. They are paid a solid living wage, and they know it will never get higher. They take their time. If they can't have ambition or hope of success, they can at least have leisure.

The bureaucracy itself is a legacy from the British. When India was a British colony, the governors wanted the security of having all authority emanate from the top, from themselves. They gave no authority whatsoever to the Indians. A man way at the bottom of the scale could not even okay a check. He stamped it, passed it to a man who checked to see if the account existed and then passed it to a man who checked to see if there were sufficient funds in the account and then passed it to the head of the department, usually a Britisher, who checked all the figures and okayed it. It took then, and takes now, almost an hour to cash a check on one's own account in an Indian bank. An average of six or seven people to one job that could be done by one man is not uncommon. The system does employ many people, which is the only argument in its favor.

By keeping all authority out of the hands of the Indians,

the British neglected to prepare them to run their own government—a lapse which some people consider subtle revenge
for having lost a colony. The Indians are still unused to
authority and/or responsibility. Most of them know nothing
more, and care to know nothing more, than the old process
of passing everything upstairs to have the decisions made.
And until that process is changed or remodeled and stream-
lined, until the six unnecessary people for every job are put
to work in other, more productive areas of government employ, the Indian bureaucracy will remain a great obstacle in
the path of the country's progress.

Another reason the man gave for the crying inefficiency
in all areas of governmental and business operation is the
lack of technological equipment. In banks and in businesses,
where operations are already slow because of the ladder of
authority, they are slowed further by having all recording,
computing, and checking done by hand. Whereas in a modern American or European railroad station a ticket is issued
and confirmed by a machine, in Indian railroad stations
employers still use handwritten ledgers. It takes up to five
minutes to buy a ticket. The man finds the ticket, stamps it,
enters the sale in one ledger, then in another, takes the
money, writes the amount on the ticket, and finally hands it
to you. And you still haven't got a reservation, just the
ticket. From all but the largest stations (Delhi, Bombay, Calcutta) it takes seventy-two hours to confirm a reservation. A
cable requesting the reservation has to be sent to the point
of origin of the train, and an answer, also by cable, must be
received before the space is confirmed.

The question is not whether the necessary improvements
will be made, but whether they will be made fast enough.
India is outgrowing herself: her population, nearly four hun-

dred and fifty million at last count, increases by more than ten million every year—this in a country less than half the size of the United States. Her supply of foreign currencies, which is one of her most dire needs, dwindles every year. She is growing in size, but economically she is not keeping apace of herself. And she cannot hope to achieve what the Chinese call the "great leap forward" until her people somehow manage to shake off the lethargy that decades of British rule instilled in them. India is no longer a colony, but many Indians still think of themselves as colonials.

"We are in a difficult position," said the man. "It is not a problem of changing the government and getting more food so much as a problem of changing the *people*. We have to change everyone, from clerks to government officials, have to instill in them a whole new way of thought. And if we don't succeed, we may well have on our hands one of the most complex and unsalvageable economic, social, and political disasters in recent history. We will not be able to maintain our industry, we will not be able to defend ourselves, and most important, we will not be able to feed our people. We will gradually lose our independence by becoming more and more dependent on other countries for food and protection." He leaned back in his chair and folded his hands under his chin. "Do you know what India is?" he said. "India is a balloon, a balloon that grows daily nearer to bursting. And if she bursts, God knows what will happen to the rest of the world."

The audience with Nehru that we had was part of the prime minister's daily program. Every morning, on his way to the office, he held a half-hour reception in his house. Mostly, the people given passes were those who wished to

make a presentation of a plaque or a scroll to Pandit Nehru,
or those who had a special plea to make, or representatives
of groups who wished to state a cause or express gratitude.
Occasionally, however, foreigners such as us, with no purpose
but to meet and speak to the prime minister, were admitted.

By simple bad luck, the day we were to go turned out to
be a holiday, so more people were there than on a normal
day. We arrived at eight-thirty, and twenty or twenty-five
people, all of them Indians except one woman, were milling
around in the living room and on the terrace. We were disappointed, because a friend of ours had gotten a pass for an
odd Tuesday and had had Nehru to himself for the full half
hour.

The living room was a large rectangle of dark Indian wood,
furnished with simple, squarish couches and chairs, all up-
holstered in dark reds, dark browns, or grays. Signed photographs were on every table—Churchill, Roosevelt, Stalin,
Kennedy, every major political figure of the last twenty years.
A life-size head-and-shoulders portrait of Gandhi hung over
the door that led upstairs to Nehru's living quarters.

As we stood looking at the pictures and gazing idly around
the room, a short, stout woman in a green sari came up to us
and asked our names. We told them to her, and she checked
them against a list. Then she asked us where in the United
States we were from, where we had gone to school, and what
we were doing in India, all of which information she scribbled beside our names on the list. She thanked us, told us
she was Nehru's private secretary, and moved off to talk to
the others. As she passed by the groups of Indians, they all
gave her the Indian sign of respectful greeting—palms together, fingers pointed upward in a prayerful gesture, a
slight bow with the upper body. She smiled benignly and

nodded. When she had spoken to everyone in the room, she went out through a door at the far end of the rectangle and started up the stairs.

At quarter to nine, she reappeared in the doorway. She said nothing, but raised her hand. Immediately, all talk stopped. Down the stairs and through the door, walking slowly and wearing a wide, peaceful smile, came Mr. Nehru. He was dressed in a maroon jacket and white hat, and he wore a pink rose in a buttonhole. All the Indians put their hands together and bowed. We just bowed. He strolled casually through the groups of people, stopping at every one to say a few words. One group presented him with a flowered lei, which the leader, a big Sikh, put around his head. Nehru bowed, thanked the man, and took the lei off and gave it to an attendant. The only other non-Indian, a European woman, stopped Nehru as he moved through the crowd, and in halting English made a plea for his support of a school project in the Benares area. He said that he would do everything he could to help the woman, asked her how she liked India, and moved on. She tried to pursue the matter further, but he was already speaking to someone else.

He seemed to know a few of the visitors, and he stopped to chat with them about their families or their pet projects. When he lingered too long, his secretary whispered something to him and guided him to some new people. Charlie and I were sure he'd never get to us, and we began to feel foolish standing with our hands clasped behind our backs.

He worked his way through the crowd, then turned toward us. The people between him and ourselves had already had their audience, and he nodded to them as he passed. He stopped in front of us and performed the palms-together gesture. We started to respond in kind, but he recognized our uneasiness with it, and held out his hand instead. "Harvard, eh?" he said.

"Yes, sir," we said in unison.

"How do you like India?"

"It's fascinating," I said.

"We haven't been here very long, only a couple of days," said Charlie.

He smiled. There was a pause, and Charlie and I both struggled for something to say. Before coming, we had prepared questions that we were going to ask if we got him alone. I was going to ask him about Menon's role in shaping India's foreign policy, Charlie was going to ask something about India and the neutral countries as a group, and there were three or four other questions that we held in reserve in case we had time to raise them. We couldn't think of any of them.

Suddenly Charlie spoke up. "Sir," he said, "I'd like to ask you a question. I'm going into politics, and I've got this chance to go around the world. What would you suggest that I concentrate on, what should I learn, what should I try most to appreciate?"

Nehru looked stunned. "Well," he said slowly, "all politics are based on economics. The first thing that a man should have for politics is a solid background in economics. Also, it is always terribly important to search out the truth in every situation. Unfortunately, much depends on geography, on who your neighbors are."

I said, "But we've found, sir, that there never really is any absolute truth in a given situation. There seem always to be two sides to every question, and to an observer who lacks intimate knowledge of a situation, the two sides don't instruct as much as they confuse."

"There are even more than two sides," said Nehru. "There are often a great many sides to a question, a great many facets that must be taken into account in searching for each particular truth. But in searching for all truths, it's important always to try to look at the problem from the other man's point of view. The most important thing is an understanding. One must try to understand the other man's position."

"But—"

His secretary whispered to him. He bowed, shook hands, and said, "Enjoy your stay in India." He turned away and walked over to someone else.

It was, of course, impossible for us to form any definite impression of the man, for we had had too little time with him, and neither Charlie nor I had had a chance to relax and think about what he was saying. But if one quality of the man did come across more than any others, it was his serenity. In his face, in his whole demeanor, there was nothing but calm. He smiled or he did not smile, he spoke or he did not speak, yet there was never a real change of expression. His voice was soft, and what he said always appeared to have been thought out, mulled over, and released from somewhere deep inside him to float to the surface. There was nothing hurried about anything he said or did. We felt that his vitality was all far within him, to be spent not on us but on his thoughts.

At exactly nine-fifteen, he was escorted to the front door of the house. He turned and bowed to the people in the living room, then walked out of the house and got in his car.

We had been in India almost a week and had met not one Indian girl. We had met wives of friends and sons of friends but never daughters of friends. Finally, one night at dinner, a man introduced us to his daughter, and she asked us to visit her school, in Delhi University, and said she would introduce us to her friends.

We met the girl after one of her classes, and she led us around behind the building, where ten or fifteen girls and two or three boys sat on the ground in a circle. We were introduced all around and told to sit wherever we could find a place. Charlie walked to the other side of the circle and squeezed in between two young girls. I sat beside a lovely girl in a blue and gold sari.

For the first few minutes, the conversation was a political symposium. One person spoke at a time, and when he was through, someone else either disagreed with him or elaborated on what he had said. They fired questions about America at us one after another, and Charlie and I passed the buck back and forth until one or the other of us said something that made a bit of sense. Slowly, the group began to split up into smaller conversational groups, and to my delight I found myself talking to the girl in the blue and gold sari. She was very formal, though not cold.

"What interests you most about India?" she said.

"Social customs," I said.

"What social customs in particular?"

I released the first test signal. "Mostly among young people," I said. "I'm interested in knowing how customs have changed, how much tradition still remains, and how Indian customs differ from European customs. For instance, at what age do girls start going out in India?"

"Going out?" said the girl. "What do you mean, 'going out'?"

"Seeing young men on their own. Going to films or plays, or even just having dinner with young men."

"I see what you mean," she said. "No, in India girls do not 'go out,' as you say."

"Never? Not at all?"

"No."

"Then how do they get to know the person they're going to marry?"

"They don't, usually. That is not important."

"You mean they just marry the first person that comes along?"

She laughed. "No, of course not. It is all arranged by the parents."

"I see. So you never even meet the person you're going to marry."

"Certainly we do! Times have changed since the days when a girl met her husband at the wedding for the first time. Nowadays a girl sees her husband at least two or three times before they get married."

"Grand," I said. "That makes all the difference. But suppose you don't like him? What do you do then?"

"You tell your parents that you don't like him, and often your parents will find you someone else. But that happens very rarely. Most of the time the parents pick well."

"And what about you? When are you getting married?"

"I don't know," she said. "When I finish school, I guess."

"Do you know who you're going to marry?"

"Of course not. That's still more than a year away."

"Have your parents picked him yet?"

"I don't know. I haven't asked them. I imagine they have someone in mind."

"What about a little thing called love?"

"What do you mean, 'love'? If your parents have chosen well, then as you live with your husband you learn to respect him and understand him. You have mutual interests—

again, if your parents have chosen well—and mutual tastes. You are, if you will, compatible."

"Is there never any romantic love, any of that feeling that you can't live without someone, that every minute you're away is painful and every minute you're together is wonderful? Haven't you ever felt that way about someone?"

She smiled. Her face was beautiful—dark eyes, a fine, straight nose, thin lips, and straight black hair that fell down to her shoulders in a long braid. "That is a silly notion," she said. "It is inconceivable to me."

I paused for a moment, then said, "Has an Indian girl ever married a Frenchman?"

"I guess so, at one time or other. Two years ago, a friend of mine married an Englishman. She claimed that she felt this love you speak of. I even remember her phrase for it: she said to me, 'I'm madly in love with him.' All her friends thought she was crazy."

"Is she happy now?"

"I haven't heard from her."

"What about sex?" I said. "Is there no love in—"

"Please," she said. "Let us not talk about sex. One does not."

We spent the rest of the hour talking about America's reasons for not admitting Red China to the U.N.

In the taxi back to town, Charlie said, "And how did *you* make out?"

"Miserably. Yourself?"

"Jeezeree! I mentioned one thing about going out with members of the opposite sex, and you'd have thought I was asking her if she slept with her brother, the way she reacted. Wouldn't say another word to me."

That night we walked past a Parsee wedding ceremony.

Crowds of people were standing around eating ice cream and drinking soda, and the orchestra was playing "Itsy Bitsy Teeny Weeny Yellow Polka Dot Bikini."

I said, "There's your mysterious East for you."

"Never mind," replied Charlie. "Those *girls* are sure mysterious."

12

AFTER ten days in New Delhi, we knew we had to get out. We had seen the sights and had seen all the people we had access to, and we had fallen into the rut of doing nothing but reading *Time* and going to American movies. We might as well have been in New Rochelle. Also, as much as the heat made us reluctant to move anywhere, we knew that only by going into the countryside could we see India. Delhi is tourist-oriented, and so are the people.

("Baksheesh, sa'ab, give me one rupee. No mama, no papa. Give me one rupee. Wait, sa'ab. I tell your fortune."

"No."

"What you say if I tell your mother's name?"

"No."

"Only five rupees, sa'ab. No charge if I don't tell your mother's name. If I do it, then you let me tell fortune."

"You can't tell me my mother's name."

"Here, sa'ab, hold piece of paper."

A little sleight of hand, and a dollar is gone, for which you have found that you will be given fifty thousand dollars, that a blond girl will change your life, and that you must be on the lookout for a red-haired man named Jim who is up to no good.)

We had heard that the Peace Corps had a group of twenty-six workers in India, and that they were stationed in Ludhiana, a town in the Punjab some hundred and fifty miles north of Delhi. We tried to arrange a visit, but the American Embassy could do nothing for us, and recommended that we just go up and try to see them. The office of the Peace Corps in Delhi could not provide help, either, for if they did anything for us, they would then have to provide service for every tourist. We would have to go on our own, and leave any hospitality to the discretion of the individual representatives.

The trip to Ludhiana is overnight on the train, through dry, dusty, flat country. We were told to lock our compartment door, for in stations and at water stops the locals are prone to climbing in and making off with whatever they find. We were also advised not to allow anyone to sleep on our floor, which people often ask to do, for every year a few people are murdered and/or robbed by the seemingly decrepit old men to whom they have extended this harmless courtesy. And we were told not to drink water on the train or eat the food on the station platforms, since there is no point in getting dysentery any sooner than is absolutely necessary. Later, after traveling extensively and healthily on trains throughout India, we would get cocky and start eating station food, to our great and prolonged discomfort. In all fairness to the opposite school of thought, there are those who believe that you might as well eat and drink everything everywhere, because you're going to get sick sooner or later, and the sooner you do get sick, the less suspense you have to go through as to when you *are* going to get sick. Again, that's the other school of thought. But one of its more illustrious advocates was Ambassador Galbraith, so perhaps there's something to it.

We arrived in Ludhiana at six-thirty in the morning, and were immediately set upon by ranks of bicycle rickshaws, the local taxis. Finally, after each of our mothers had been cursed, had the milk of her mother cursed, and had every child until her next incarnation spat upon, we fell into two rickshaws and told the drivers to take us to a hotel. Our intent was not to stay in a hotel, but, hopefully, to find a concierge who spoke English and could direct us to Peace Corps headquarters. We tried three hotels—one above a fish market, one behind a fruit market, and the Grand Hotel—before we found a man who could speak English. But he didn't know what the Peace Corps was, and he directed us to the post office. Finally, at eight-thirty, we were deposited, panting in the ninety-degree heat, at the Peace Corps barracks.

We were met by the head of the group, a young man of about twenty-three, named Paul Winther. We told him that we had come up to see them and that we wondered if we could talk to them or perhaps even see what they were doing. Paul said that not only could we see them work, but they would put us up and feed us for a couple of days if we wanted to stay. They had some extra bicycles, and he said we could go out that afternoon with one member of the group who was going from village to village talking to the people. The group had not been there long (two or three months), and they were still trying to get acquainted with and gain the confidence of the people. We put our suitcases inside and changed our clothes, and he showed us around the barracks and told us what their life was like. He wouldn't describe the work they were doing, since he said we'd get a chance to see that for ourselves.

The barracks, a two-story white frame house, served as headquarters for the twenty-six Peace Corps representatives in India. They are, or were in March of 1962, all in the Punjab—some in Amritsar, some in Chandigarh, some moving from town to town. Only six or seven actually lived at the Ludhiana barracks, and of those, two or three spent the week nights in the surrounding villages. Whenever possible, groups from the other towns spent their weekends in Ludhiana. The barracks were sparsely furnished, with iron bunks, one toilet and one shower. When we were there, all washing was done at an outside pump, since something was wrong with the bathroom plumbing.

Facilities for entertainment simply did not exist. The province is dry except for a low-proof beer. There are no English-language films north of Delhi. All books must be specially shipped up from Delhi. Since time-honored Indian customs stringently regulate the social activities of young women, the Peace Corps group cannot even indulge in the major Indian pastime, sex (called Poor Man's Polo), which is the only entertainment Indians in that area have and which is one of the reasons why India's population grows at such an alarming rate. There was one woman among the twenty-six Peace Corps representatives, and she was married to another member of the Corps in the Punjab. So most of the days began and ended early, and consisted almost entirely of work, either with the Indian people or around the barracks.

We carried lunch with us, two sandwiches and some fruit, and Charlie and I, led by a boy named Arthur, started out on bicycles. The villages we were going to visit were on the other side of Ludhiana, so we had to pass through the town. The barracks was about a mile from the center of Ludhiana, and as we went along the paved road, Arthur explained his job to us. Unlike most of the others in the group, he was not a farmer, nor was he trained in any technical or industrial field. He had had some agricultural training, but not enough to qualify him to work with farmers on specific problems. Instead, for the first few months he had had to try to get to know the people of the villages and their problems—how their school systems worked and what could be done to improve them, how the villages were organized, what they needed, what interests and needs and desires the people had, and on and on *ad infinitum*. He had to learn the customs of the Punjab, and if he could, learn the language. In a few weeks he had mastered the simple phrases, the how-do-you-dos, the thank-yous, the farewells. He told us that the way to greet a Punjabi was to say "soc-*city*-agah."

We rode into Ludhiana. It is a large industrial town, and like all Indian towns, it is filthy and overpopulated. The food is sold at open-air markets, and flies swarm over everything. Cows wander the streets, people throw garbage wherever they feel like throwing it, and from morning till night the streets are jammed with masses of aimless, shuffling humanity. There are very few cars, but many trucks and innumerable bicycles. The sound of frantically ringing bicycle bells stands out above all others. It is usually impossible to ride a bicycle on the main streets—the crowds are too thick. On the side streets, one must ride with one hand on the brake, the other on the bell, for everyone rides fast, and pedestrians are sluggishly unconcerned about their own well-being. We had been told that for drivers of automobiles, the hit-and-run philosophy is the only way to survive, which did not cheer us.

Outside of town, we traveled on paved roads for about a mile, then turned off onto dirt tracks. It is all farm country, largely wheat, and irrigated by rivers. Little of the land is planted, and where there are not cultivated fields, the land is parched and barren. The villages are small and close together, no more than a mile or two apart. The houses are brick or mud or clay, or a combination of all three. They are small and sparsely furnished.

In the distance, we heard a machine working with a strange sound, a hollow "pokapokapokapoka," and we asked Arthur what it was. A diesel pump, he said, and the reason the noise was so loud was that the owner of such a device was terribly proud of it and replaced the muffler with an echo can so it could be heard, his status symbol, all around the neighboring countryside.

We stopped at a school in a village named Gill. The principal, a tall, bearded Sikh wearing a white turban and a faded blue blazer, came to greet us. He smiled warmly at Arthur and put his palms together, fingers pointing upward, bowed, and said, "Soc-*city*-agah." Arthur replied, and introduced us to the principal and the teachers, and we had soc-*city*-agahs all around, which amused the Indians. Then the principal showed us around the school. His English was excellent, but he and one other teacher were the only ones who spoke anything but Punjabi. The others, he said, could not even speak Hindi, which is, with English, the official language of India.

The school was a yard about thirty yards on each side, with one low building in the middle for classes, and a small stone hut for the office. The classroom building was made of stone and wood, about eight feet wide and sixty feet long, and it had no chairs, no desks, and no blackboard. The children sat on straw mats on the stone floor and faced one end, where the teacher stood. It was called a middle school, and had four classes, grades five through eight. There were two hundred students in the school, taught by seven teachers, the principal among them. They were taught Punjabi, mathematics, and "general knowledge"—which included such subjects as geography and reading. In the sixth or seventh grade, they began Hindi and English.

When we had seen the school, the principal invited us into his office for tea. The office was furnished with a desk and three chairs. It was small, perhaps six feet by eight, and one window was cut into the stone wall. The principal sat at his desk, and Arthur, Charlie, and I sat in the three chairs. The teachers stood by the desk. Outside, the whole school gathered around the hut, and the children giggled and tittered and shoved one another until one of the teachers went out and silenced them. Ten cups were laid out, and a drink which was half tea and half milk was served from a tin can.

As is customary, the conversation began with standard platitudes—Charlie and I: "We are here to learn."

Arthur: "The eyes of the world are on India."

The Principal: "America has always shown brotherhood and friendship to India."

Arthur: "The youth of today are the leaders of tomorrow."

Then we talked about the school. They needed books, he said, books and writing implements. The thought of a reasonable physical plant for the school was so obviously impossible that it was never brought up. Instead, he asked once about the physical layout of a comparable school in

America. He said he would like to go to America, but what little money he saved went to support his parents. He was the last son, so that was his duty. He had once tried to go to America, but the wait for the visa was too long. Besides, he felt he was doing more for his country where he was. There are too few teachers in India, he said, and he felt sure that education was the only thing that could make her a truly independent, self-sufficient country. It was a start, at least. A country that wishes to progress cannot let half its people spend their lives in total ignorance.

The serious discussion over, the principal asked us to sing an American song. We three conferred, and found that except for the first verse of "Row, row, row your boat . . ." the only song we knew in common was "Dixie." And Charlie was the only one who was sure of that. We plunged, only to find that our three voices were in conflicting ranges, so after less than one verse, the words of which I reversed, we gave up on "Dixie." The principal and the teachers smiled politely, and then, at a nod from the principal, a young teacher sat on a corner of the desk and began tapping out a quick, complicated rhythm with his right hand.

I am not a lover of Indian music. My musical tastes are relatively unsophisticated, and in vocal music I am too used to a melody line and a recognizable rhythm to readily accept the sort of free form approach of the Orientals. But what this young man sang was exquisite. He had a light, high voice that sounded impossibly delicate. The words were not sharply formed, but rather caressed by his lips. He sang a song about the Punjab, accompanying himself with the intricate rhythms his right hand tapped out on the desk. We couldn't understand a word, but there was such gentleness about the way he sang, that whatever he was saying, we were prepared to believe him. It is the only song about a country, the only national or regional anthem, I've ever heard that gets its message across softly and with feeling without blaring itself out, without bombast.

When the teacher finished, the principal asked us if we would sing a typical popular song of America, something many people know that is not an anthem or, as he phrased it, "a political song." Arthur denied knowledge of any. I thought of becoming suddenly mute, when Charlie spoke up and said that he and I had a smashing version of "Funny Valentine" that we'd love to do. We began, with Charlie improvising here and there and I reaching for notes I never knew existed, and somehow we got through it. The Indians, to whom this music was as strange as theirs was to us, were cordial. I don't think we moved them.

We talked for a few minutes more, and then went out and had our pictures taken with the students and teachers. A few more platitudes—

Arthur: "Education is progress."

The Principal: "Your open hearts are an inspiration to us."

Charlie and I: "Right."

—and we rode off down the dusty path.

During the afternoon, we stopped at two or three more villages, and at each one the procedure was the same: platitudes, tea, serious talk, jollity, more platitudes. We were always most hospitably received, and the villagers were often proud to show us their tiny houses.

On the way back to Ludhiana, I asked Arthur if our afternoon had accomplished anything in terms of Peace Corps work. He said it had. For the first few months, his only task would be to get the people to know and trust him, to learn that they could talk to him as a friend. All the formality, all the bromides, were simply a part of the Indian process of making friends. At first, he said, their conversations had been nothing but bromides. Then, gradually, he found he could talk about more concrete things, and now the platitudes came only at the beginning and end of their meetings. Eventually, he hoped, the formality would disappear entirely, and he would be able to come and go in the villages without causing a flurry of bowing and politeness. Then he would be accepted, and only then could he really begin to help them, to advise them and believe that they would take his advice.

That night for dinner we had chicken and milk and Jello. The group ate Indian cooking one day, American the next, and we were lucky enough to be there for the American night. We had had curry twice a day for so long that anything not bathed in spice was a relief. After dinner, we talked for a few minutes, and then went to bed. Charlie and I flipped for the only available pillow, and he won, so I rolled up a blanket and put it under my head. The night was cool, and we slept soundly, each secretly congratulating himself for actually having accomplished something during the day.

We were awakened early by someone calling us. We ran upstairs to the porch, and there was the whole group gathered at the rail, looking off to the northeast. "The Himalayas," said Paul, pointing. "You can see them only on very clear mornings, and even then only early in the morning. As soon as the heat begins to rise, they're lost."

I looked across the dry, flat plains, and for a moment all I could see were tiny clouds on the horizon. Then, slowly, the clouds began to take shape; each one was the sharp, pinkish-white top of a snow-covered mountain. They seemed to glow against the crisp blue of the early morning sky, a hundred, two hundred miles away. The line of peaks seemed endless, miniscule spikes on the horizon that disappeared off to the north and curved out of sight to the east. It was not that you could see some of them and not others, the farthest ones, but rather that the farther away the peaks were, the more they looked like small clouds, until you were sure that the farthest away couldn't be mountains.

We went inside and had cornflakes and tangerines.

Roger Engstrom is a farmer from Iowa. He had been working on his father's farm when he got the idea of joining the Peace Corps. He had never traveled much, and he thought this might be a way to see the world. Also, he was interested in seeing how other people farmed. And he knew that with his knowledge of fertilizers, modern farming techniques, and of the land, he could be of some help to these people. Roger is the ideal Peace Corps representative. He is well-trained, interested, dedicated. He has grown up in the country and is used to country living. He does not pine for the theater, for movies, for magazines or books. He derives a great deal of pleasure from nature. He is kind, relatively uncomplicated, and direct. And perhaps most important of all, he is patient.

There were five of us—Roger, Arthur, an Indian supervisor for agricultural affairs of the area, Charlie and myself. We rode through Ludhiana and started east along the paved road. Just before we left the town, I glanced to the right at a large gulch, about six feet below the level of the land, a hundred or so feet long and fifty feet wide. In the center of the gulch a pack of vultures flapped and clawed and

ripped away at something that was lying in their midst. All
around were the dried bones of cattle.

"It's a cow," said Roger. "The Indians won't eat the
meat, so when the things die, they throw them here for the
vultures."

I was startled. "They still stick to that no meat policy?
All of them?"

"Pretty nearly. We got a pamphlet the other day. Said
in 1956 India had one fourth of all the world's cattle—one
hundred and fifty-six million head, plus forty-four million
head of water buffalo. Damn things eat all the grain and
put a big hole in the economy. And the Indians won't eat
a one of them. They ask for grain aid instead."

"But why don't they sell them?"

"They use them for milk. When the milk runs out, they
let them run around eating garbage, so they're no good for
meat by then. Besides, there's still some religious feeling
about it. You'll never see an Indian kill a cow. Beat the
hell out of them now and then, but never kill them."

The thought was infuriating. "For God's sake, don't
they—"

"It's what they believe," said Roger, "and you can't mess
around with their beliefs. Not if you want to get anywhere
with them."

It was a long ride, and with every push on the pedals the
day got hotter. The heat rose visibly from the road, and
under every tree, groups of Indians lay in the grass. About
six miles outside Ludhiana we turned left on a rutted road.
In the distance, two houses stood in a clump of trees. As
we approached, we could see children walking in and out of
the trees, carrying trays of what looked like clay on their
heads. I asked Roger what they were doing.

"Carrying cow manure," he said. "They collect it fresh
and put it in piles to dry. It's fertilizer and fuel for them.
I've been trying to get them to bury it until they need it,
because that way they'll retain all the minerals. Now they
just set it out to dry, and all the nutrients dry out of it."

The farmyard was small. It sat on the bank of a stream
that ran a thin trickle of murky brown water past the houses.
The main house was on the right. It was long and low, two
rooms, a kitchen and a bedroom–living room. Ten yards
from the house was a wall, against which fifteen head of
cattle were lying tethered out of the sun. In the center
of the yard a pile of manure patties baked in the sun. A
huge pile of fresh manure sat on the bank of the stream, and
two little girls scooped traysful and took them to the center
pile and patted it into cakes. Across the stream were the
fields.

The farmer came out to greet us. He was a tall, strong-
looking, bearded Sikh, and he wore gold-rimmed glasses.
He welcomed Roger with a warm soc-*city*-agah, then greeted
us formally, with the palms-together gesture.

"Come," he said to us. "I must show you my prize."

We walked across the yard to where a new red tractor was
standing under a tree.

"Is it fixed?" asked Roger.

"Just today," said the farmer. "I think it runs well now."
He turned to us. "You like it?"

"Beautiful," I said.

"Great," said Charlie, hoping, as did I, that these were
suitable adjectives for tractors.

"It is Polish," said the farmer. "Good machines, but very
hard to repair. When they sent them to us, they did not
send many spare parts."

"How many farmers have tractors?" asked Charlie.

"Very, very few," said Roger. "This man is one of the most successful farmers in the Punjab. He actually makes money now, about a thousand dollars a year, net, which isn't bad when you consider that the average per capita annual income in India is sixty-six dollars. Most farmers have to eat a lot of what they produce, and trade the rest for clothes."

Roger and the farmer led the way across the stream into the fields.

"Look at this wheat," he said. It looked just like regular wheat to me. "This is fine wheat, tall, big, and very healthy. You see how close together it grows, how many stalks in, say, a square foot. On fifty acres this man grows more than twice as much wheat as his neighbor, who has a hundred and fifty acres."

"How?"

"He uses modern fertilizers and chemicals, builds up the land instead of letting it use itself up after a year or two. What I'm trying to do is get the other farmers in the area to follow his example. I think we're inching forward a little bit, but my God, it's a slow process."

"Why? Don't they see what can be done? And if so, why don't they do it?"

"Take this man's neighbor for an example," said Roger. We were walking along a strip of border land between the two properties. "Now look at *this* wheat." We looked, and there was indeed a difference. The wheat was thin and short, and where the first farmer had fifty stalks, this man had perhaps fifteen, and they were sickly. "I'll tell you about our crusade with this guy," he said, pointing to the wheat.

When the group first arrived, Roger had searched for one

farmer who was using new methods. He had found him, the man whose farm we were visiting, and had helped him further, suggesting new devices and new fertilizers. His premise was that since this man was admired by the other farmers, they might be persuaded to try the same methods. Roger went to the farm nearby and talked to the farmer there. The conversation had gone something like this:

"I cannot afford to buy all the fertilizers you suggest," said the farmer. "I make barely enough to feed my family as it is."

"I understand that, sir," said Roger, "but if you start little by little, trying the new materials on even one acre, your production will gradually rise, and you will be able to afford more."

"But suppose I put all this money into it, and it doesn't work. Where am I then?"

"But it *will* work. Don't you see what it did for your neighbor?"

"It worked for him, but how can you guarantee that it will work for me?"

"I assure you, sir, it will work."

"How do I know that? Suppose it doesn't. Then I'm without all that money. Besides, suppose the locusts come again, as they did three years ago. What then? Can you keep the locusts away?"

"No, I can't."

"So I put all the money into it, even if it does work, and the locusts come and eat me out. If they come now, it is bad enough. But how much worse if I spend more money on the crop! If you give me the fertilizers, I will try them."

"I can't afford to give you all the fertilizers, but if you buy them, I'll help you with them."

"So I must take your word that they will work, spend all

the money, and get no guarantee. No. I cannot do that. I am not a rich man."

"I can do one thing," said Roger. "If you lend me one strip of your land, a small one, I'll buy fertilizer and chemicals for it, and I'll plant it myself. Then you can see if it works or not."

The farmer thought for a moment. "But if it does not work, then I am without the crop from that land. I cannot afford to waste any crop."

"But it will work. I'm not asking you to give me your land, only to let me plant it in a new way, so you can see for yourself."

"I will think about it," said the farmer.

Four days later the farmer agreed, and Roger set about planting the strip of land.

"Now," said Roger, "we have to wait and see if he'll take up the example and buy his own when this one works. He may just sit back and be happy with the little extra the strip will bring him. He's got another problem I'm working on now. A lot of his land is practically useless because of a huge salt deposit. The land has been mistreated for so long that it has all become too salty. I could get rid of the salt in a matter of weeks, but we go through the same rigmarole. I have to supply and plant the first chemicals, prove to him I'm not trying to cut his throat, before he'll even think about trying something new."

"I'd go nuts," said Charlie. "Don't you get frustrated?"

"It's hard," said Roger. "They have four crops a year here, where we have one, and they could produce God knows how many times more than they do. But," he shrugged his shoulders and smiled, "you can't blame them, really. A stranger walks in and tells them he's going to help them, if only they'll shell out a lot of money they don't have. I know

I'd be wary if someone came to me with a proposition like that. I'd think he was some sort of carpetbagger."

We made a five-mile circle of the farms in the area, skidding and falling on the ruts in the narrow dirt roads. At each farm, we were offered (and had to accept) a cup of the milk-tea mixture. And at each farm we went through five minutes of platitudes. Before we turned back toward the main road, Roger stopped us in front of eight long rows of watermelons. We walked down the second row and stood near the end. Elsewhere in the row the plants were well up. Here they had barely begun.

"This is another beauty," said Roger. "All the farmers have always used compost as fertilizer for the watermelons. It's the best you can get, and it's done a good job for them. But somehow one man got hold of all the compost supplies for the area, and now he sits on his ass in Ludhiana and controls prices. He can get whatever he asks, of course, and what he asks is about twice what the stuff is worth—easily twice what the farmers can comfortably afford. But they have to buy from him."

"Isn't there anything else they can use?" asked Charlie.

"Yes, and here's the problem. I went to the watermelon farmer and told him I could suggest certain chemical fertilizers that would do just as good a job and that would be far cheaper for him in the long run. They'd be better for the land, too. I got the same reaction the wheat farmer gave me: how do I know it will work, what guarantees can you give me? I persuaded him to give me part of one of his rows so I could prove it to him. I planted the stuff, and now the damn things aren't growing." He pointed to the tiny beginnings of the plants. "They will grow, but they'll take a little longer than the others, because for one thing, they were planted a little later. I have quite a time convincing

the farmer of that, though. He comes along and sees his
plants bigger than mine, and he immediately concludes that
my fertilizer is crummy. I don't mind that so much as that
I think he now figures I was trying to put something over on
him. If I can make him wait and reserve judgment, I may
win. If he starts parading around the countryside telling all
his neighbors that I tried to con him, then all the progress
I've made will be shot. I could show them a four-ton watermelon, and they'd spit in my eye."

That night we had an early dinner. It was Thursday, and
members of groups from other towns were beginning to arrive for the weekend. A soccer game was scheduled for Saturday, Peace Corps vs. the local engineering school, and they
hoped to have all twenty-six Peace Corps people there for
the weekend. They were setting up metal cots and Indian
webbed beds in every available corner, and someone had
been sent into Ludhiana for beer. It cost about eighty cents
a quart, so it was treated like gold.

After dinner, Roger and Paul offered to drive us into
Ludhiana on the backs of their motorbikes. We packed, and
gingerly arranged ourselves on the luggage racks, clutching
our suitcases and trying somehow to hold on. When we got
to the train station, we found that the train would be more
than an hour late. Roger and Paul refused to leave, so we
spent the hour riding the motorbikes in tight circles around
the station. This was stopped when I got arrested for going
the wrong way through an alley, and the Peace Corps's reputation was only saved from the ignominy of being discovered
with as yet unregistered vehicles by a lot of talk and someone
offering to buy the policeman a cup of tea. He laughed, and
we had many soc-*city*-agahs, and Charlie and I got on the
train.

That night an old man asked if he could sleep on the floor

of our compartment. He was a very polite, nice-looking old man, and we were sorry to have to refuse.

Later, Charlie and I talked often of the Peace Corps representatives we had met, and the more we talked, the more we realized that they are truly an impressive lot. These are people who are giving up a great deal: time, money, comfort, fun, relaxation, and whatever luxury most Americans can afford. They are away from their families and their friends, away from language and customs that have been the most basic of securities all their lives.

Materially, the returns are meager. The salary, most of which is saved for them, is small, about a thousand dollars a year. But they are fed and sheltered and supplied with whatever tools they need. They have an opportunity to travel when their tour of duty is over, and most of that travel will be paid for by the government. Aside from those rewards, no one can say what each individual gets out of his two years. He learns a great deal about many things, about new people, new thoughts, a new way of life. But how he matures, what sense of accomplishment he feels, how his life will be changed when he returns, all these are the variables.

Regardless of anything else he may feel, the Peace Corps representative has a right to be proud. Not all of what he has accomplished is tangible, but all of it is important. If he has helped one farmer to have a better life, that in itself is enough to be proud of. If he has, as he hopes, shown a group of people how to support themselves, how to be independent of other people's aid, all the better. But he is doing more. He is educating people, and thus releasing them from the vicious slavery that ignorance imposes.

13

Even before we left the United States, Charlie and I had agreed on one thing: no matter where in the world we went, no matter if our route took us over Mongolia and the North Pole, we were eventually going to get to an island in the South Seas, a "tropical paradise," where we could loll on a white beach beneath swaying palms and fish for our dinner on the coral reefs, where we could commune with nature and cleanse ourselves of the scales of civilization.

Charlie's first thought was Tahiti, but I, displaying worldly wisdom acquired from a magazine article, told him that because of jet travel, new hotels had sprung up, pictures were being filmed there, and the island was nothing like what he imagined it to be. Bora-Bora, the island near Tahiti, was better, more natural, but even it was uttering its death rattle as a tropical paradise and undergoing a rebirth as a child of the age of Hilton.

One night I was looking through a copy of *Horizon,* and I found a piece about the five last unspoiled areas in the world. Picture after picture showed lush tropical islands with white sand beaches and swaying palms, but most of them were more than a thousand dollars' flight out of our way. Then suddenly I saw our place. A full-page color picture showed the most beautiful beach I had ever seen, with white sand, curling breakers, and the bluest water in the world, on the edge of a rich, green jungle. The caption told us that the name of the place was Galle, on the southern tip of Ceylon and well within our reach.

However hot it got in India and Pakistan, however much we suffered through dust and dirt and discomfort, we were always buoyed by the thought of Galle, with its clear skies and gentle breezes. We were like Buddhists trudging through life with only one goal, Nirvana, when every care would cease and the milk and honey would start to flow.

When we landed in Ceylon, it was a hundred and ten and humid. We stumbled off the plane into the airport bus, and collapsed for the hour's ride into Colombo. "Some tropical paradise," said Charlie.

"Don't give up yet," I said. "Look out the window." Even here on the outskirts of the capital of the country, there were deep jungles and thatched huts and mango and banana trees. And if we looked closely, we could see the sea through the trees. As soon as we got to the hotel, we went downstairs to make plans to go to Galle.

Galle itself, said the concierge, had no beach: it was a fishing town, mostly walled in, with some narrow strips of sand beach, but not many. Where we wanted to go was Hik-kaduwa, next to Galle.

"The name isn't important," said Charlie. "We'll take it."

"There is one problem," said the concierge. "I don't think you can get a reservation."

"Reservation?" I said. "Reservation for what, the beach?"

"No. There's only one place to stay, a government rest-house, and it's usually full."

"We can sleep in a shack," said Charlie. "We don't need a hotel or a resthouse."

"A shack? Where are you going to find a shack?"

Charlie shrugged. "I don't know. Maybe one of the natives will rent us one."

"Rent you his home? That's all they have, you know. It's a small, poor village. Anyway, you wouldn't want to live in one of their houses."

"Why not?"

"They're small and hot and dirty, and they have no lights and no screens."

"Then we'll sleep on the beach," I said.

"Not bloody likely," said the concierge. "If you slept on the beach with your luggage, you'd be lucky to wake up in the morning, and luckier still to wake up and find anything left. Even if you left your bags here and took nothing that anyone would want to steal, you couldn't sleep on the beach. You'd be up every ten seconds swatting at an insect—or at a cloud of insects, more likely."

I said, "You don't seem to be very anxious for us to go there."

"It's not that," said the concierge. "It's just that if you are going to go, you must realize that you'll have to live like civilized beings. 'Back to nature' and all that is very nice, but not very practical."

The next morning the concierge told us that because of a

sudden cancellation, he had been able to secure us one of the ten rooms in the resthouse for three days.

The train ride south to Hikkaduwa was two hours long, and the scenery was exquisite. The tracks ran along the shore, some fifty or sixty yards from the water. On our right, through the trees, was the sea. On our left, not five feet from the tracks, was the jungle. We passed by several small villages—clusters of thatched huts, outrigger canoes lying on the beach, children wrapped in gaily colored cloth running through the jungle.

"Man, this is it," said Charlie dreamily as he stared out the window. "This is what the South Seas should be like."

Still, it was hot, over a hundred, and humid, so when we arrived at the resthouse, which was clean and pleasant and beautifully situated on a small point of land, we threw off our clothes, put on our bathing suits, and rushed for the water. At the edge of the shore, a sign read, "Swimming not permitted here—strong currents, sharp coral." We were advised to swim in a tiny area at the crotch of the point of land. It was a small tidal pool, perhaps ten yards across, protected from the currents. We decided against that, and walked a few hundred yards down the beach. We were hot and tired and sticky and dirty, and when we found a place where there seemed to be no dangerous coral, we raced each other into the water.

It was like falling into yesterday's bath water. If the air was a hundred and ten, the water was ninety. It was clear and clean and sparkling, but it felt syrupy and dirty. It gave no relief from the heat, but rather coated us with salt and made us itch. We wallowed in it for a few minutes, just because it was water and we knew that even if it didn't feel clean, it would remove some of the grime. We tried to ride some of the larger waves, but they were the kind that break sharply and have no roll, so they picked us straight up in the air and dropped us onto the small pieces of rock and coral that were scattered about in the sand. We crawled out of the water and lay down on the beach. Within two minutes we began to sweat, and the sweat attracted bugs. We got up and walked back to the resthouse, where we took showers in tepid chlorinated water.

We were told that the ocean cooled down in the late afternoon, so while we waited, we decided to take a walk through the jungle in back of the resthouse. A small path began across the road. We put on shirts, hoping to keep some of the bugs away, and started off.

The path was full of roots and stones, and before we had gone fifty feet we wished that we had worn shoes. We had to keep our eyes on the ground, so as not to cut our feet, and the only way we could see where we were was to stop. The air in the jungle was heavy and wet. When we passed the shacks, the women who were washing clothes in brown water or beating them clean on rocks would stop work and stare at us.

But the jungle was beautiful. We stopped by a large rock and sat down to rest our feet and let the sweat dry, hoping the quick evaporation would cool us. The colors were spectacular, bougainvillaea and mangoes and ten thousand fruits and flowers that we had never heard of. Monkeys chattered and played in the trees, and birds, cawing and cackling, fluttered about far overhead, as the sunlight that seeped in between the tops of the trees played on their orange and yellow and red wings. Dark-skinned boys with gleaming white teeth laughed and chased each other among the shacks. Despite the noises of the animals, it was peaceful, and if the heat was uncomfortable, the colors were soothing.

We started off again, carefully placing one foot in front

of the other, feeling for rocks. Suddenly I heard a tittering behind us, and I turned to see a group of ten or fifteen children who had been noiselessly following us. They walked easily on their calloused feet, not bothering about stones, and every time Charlie or I winced or jumped or cursed at another bruise, they laughed merrily. They followed us, laughing at our tender feet, until we had circled the village and were back on the road by the resthouse. Now and then we looked back at them, and as soon as they saw our faces, they screamed with laughter.

It was the next afternoon, and we were sitting under a small awning, sipping bad Indian gin and watching the sun set. "You know," I said, "I think I've found out what our problem is with this place."

"What's that?" said Charlie.

"It's too much of a tropical paradise. It's exactly what we were looking for, and now that we've found it, we can't cope with it."

"How do you mean?"

"Our complaint here is that we're bored, right? There's nothing to do. We can't fish because we don't have the equipment and there's no place to rent it. The same for skindiving. There are no surfboards, no waterskis, no sailboats, no books, no movies, none of the things that we're used to having to keep us busy. We're not used to doing nothing. Look what we did today, for instance. We got up, had breakfast, and went for a swim before the water got too warm. Then we lay on the beach. Then we sat on the rocks. Then we went for another swim. Then we lay on the beach. Then we had lunch. Then we had a nap. Then we went for another swim. Then we lay on the beach. Then we sat on the rocks. Pretty exciting. What we really wanted was a place that *is* spoiled, a place that looks unchanged but that has, hidden among the trees, aqualungs, waterskis, sailboats, movie theaters, saloons, nightclubs, and dance bands. I think what we were looking for was a place that combined the advantages of civilization with the advantages of the 'tropical paradise' without the drawbacks of either."

"You know who thought of all this before you?" said Charlie. "Conrad Hilton and his cronies. All they need is a few people like us, who think we can go back to nature and then find that we need a few of the diversions of civilization, and bam! they've made a pile."

"Yeah, and—"

"Excuse me," said a voice behind us. "You are Americans, no?"

We stood up and saw a Ceylonese boy about eighteen standing just outside the awning. He was wearing a starched white shirt, a black tie, and a dark gray suit, the first such clothes we had seen since we left Colombo. Charlie and I were still in bathing suits.

"Yes," I said. "Come in and sit down."

The boy drew up a chair and sat stiffly on the edge of it, his hands folded in his lap. "I saw you on the beach today," he said.

"Do you live here?" asked Charlie.

"No, in Galle, a few miles down the road. I was visiting a relative." There was an uneasy silence as all three of us tried to think of something to say. Then the boy said to Charlie, "Do you like it here?"

"Yes," said Charlie. "It's fine."

"Oh. I see." The boy paused. He unfolded his hands and looked at his fingernails, then folded them again. He cleared his throat. "Can you help me go to America?" he said suddenly. He smiled nervously and picked at a fingernail.

"Help you in what way?" said Charlie.

"Can you get me a scholarship in America? If I can get a scholarship, they will give me a visa."

The boy was obviously embarrassed, and his embarrassment made Charlie uneasy. "No," he said, more curtly than he had intended. "It's impossible. I don't see how I can help you."

"I see," said the boy.

"Look," said Charlie, trying to make up for his harshness, "have you tried the American Embassy? Have you applied anywhere?"

"Not yet," said the boy. "Not in America. I have been given a scholarship to Lumumba Friendship University in Moscow."

"Omigod," said Charlie under his breath. "Well, that's a good school."

"Yes," said the boy, "but I don't want to go there. I want to go to America."

"I wish I could do something," said Charlie, "but I don't see how I can."

"Can't you ask Mr. Kennedy for me?"

"I'm afraid I don't know Mr. Kennedy. And even if I did, I'm not sure he could make a special exception for you."

The boy was silent. Finally, he said, "I see," and stood up. "Thank you for your time." He bowed and walked away.

"I'm sorry," said Charlie, but the boy didn't hear him, or if he did, he didn't acknowledge the apology.

Charlie sat for a moment without saying anything. Then he shook his head and said, "He changed his clothes for us, too. He went to all that trouble to impress us, and look where it got him. We couldn't help him a goddam bit."

14

In Bombay, the P & O ships on the eastern runs fill up with Indians. Some are going to Singapore to visit relatives who have businesses there, or to start businesses of their own. Some are going to Hong Kong to look for work. And some take the round trip from Bombay to Yokohama and back as their vacations. They travel tourist class, and in groups. Because India has strict regulations concerning the amount of money that may be taken out of the country, most of them have very little money to spend on amusements. Those that drink can afford only beer, and they pass the long days playing noisy card games over a glass or two of beer. The Bombay-east part of the run is never popular with the crew.

Charlie and I had embarked at Colombo, the first stop after Bombay, with tickets for Singapore, a five-day trip. The ship was the *Canton*, one of the few P & O ships that is not air-conditioned. The temperature in Colombo the day we left was between ninety-five and a hundred, and the air was heavy and wet, because it had been raining all day. The crew was irritable and impatient, and the passengers were sullen. As we threw our luggage on the bunks of our cabin on F deck, which got the heat of the engine room and the noise of the screws and whose porthole couldn't be opened except on the calmest of days because of its being so near the waterline, I wondered about the joys of liner travel.

When we were settled, I went to the dining room to arrange for our seating time for meals. The headwaiter was an old, fat, bald, sweaty Englishman with a heavy, knee-slapping sense of humor. After a few jokes, he settled down with the seating plan and tried to find places for Charlie and me.

"Would you like second sitting or first?" he said.

"Second, please."

"Lazy, what? Like to sleep late. Ha-ha. Well, let me see now. You'd like to sit with your friend, would you?"

"It's not important."

He studied his chart. "I'll be frank," he said. "I can put you together, but it'll be with a bunch of Indians, and I wouldn't do that to my worst enemy. Not even to my dog. No offense. Ha-ha."

"Why not?"

"Have you ever seen them Indians eat? Why, they eat like animals, they do. Head right in the plate. Make me spew, is what, if *I* had to sit with them."

"It doesn't make any difference," I said. "Whatever's convenient."

"Well, if that's how you want it, that's the way it'll be. Let me see, I can put you—no, no. Not there. Wouldn't think of it. I'd be crackers to put you there."

"Where?"

"Bunch of Indians. Really bad lot. Caused trouble all the way from Bombay. The captain wanted to put them off in Colombo, but the authorities didn't want any part of them."

"What did they do?"

"In my department, they just screamed and yelled and threw food. The other day, their waiter said he was going to kill one of them. They're on his back, y'know. He's a white man and all, and they love to get on a white man's back when they can. But up topside they make real trouble. Someone said they force money out of the other Indians so they can go drink at the bar. There are six of them, and I guess they just say they'll smash you if you don't come across."

The headwaiter finally found us seats at two European tables, and I scurried up to the bar. The bar was empty except for the bartender, a waiter, and a group of six Indians who sat at a table in the corner. They were playing cards and shouting across the table at one another. Two of them were big and dark—one a huge fat man, the other about six feet and stocky. The others were short and thin, with light complexions about the same color as a Caucasian with a good tan.

I sat in a chair and signaled to the waiter, who came over. He was a short, round young man with long, wavy hair and a strong Cockney twang. He was hot and tired and annoyed.

He brought me a drink, set it down, and turned to go. "Just a second," I said. "Tell me something. Who are those guys over there?"

He had been waiting for someone to ask him. He crouched down beside my chair and whispered, "Scum. Dirty, rotten, black scum. They're in here every night drinking and hollering and making trouble. If you ask me, they're all on dope,

too. Purser says he's sure, and so's the doc. Take a look at
their eyes sometime you get a chance."

"Hey, boy!" yelled one of the Indians, and the others
laughed.

"See? Ain't they charmers?" He walked over to the table.

"Six beers," said one of the two big ones. "And clear this
stuff away."

When he had served them, he came back to my chair.
"Captain should have put them off like he wanted to. Or in
irons somewhere. There's gonna be trouble with them."

We were three days out when the trouble came. Charlie
and I were in our cabin, and we heard people running in the
passageway. We looked out, and saw hordes of Indians hurrying into their cabins and shutting the doors. Curious, we
left and locked our cabin and went cautiously up the stairs.
People were gathered in small groups, talking excitedly. We
went up one more deck, to the bar. The bartender and
waiter were alone. The waiter had a cut on one cheek and
a bump on his head. We asked what had happened.

"We was here," he said, "just like normal. There was Bob
and me. The only others were a couple—a Ceylonese lad
with a club foot or one short leg or something, and his wife."
He said that the Ceylonese couple had gotten up to leave,
and as they were going out the door, three of the bad six
were coming in the door. One of them intentionally bumped
the Ceylonese man's wife, and she stumbled. The Ceylonese
man said something to the Indian, and without a word, the
Indian jumped on him and started beating him up. When
the Indian had the Ceylonese backed up against the wall, the
other two Indians pushed the cripple to the floor and started
kicking him. The bartender called out the porthole for help,
and the waiter ran over and knocked down the biggest of the

Indians. One of the others punched the waiter in the face just as two of the crew ran in the door. The Indians tried to flee, but the two crew members caught them and knocked them senseless. The man the waiter had punched made a break for the porthole, but the waiter caught him by the legs and he fell across the sill on his neck.

"Where are they now?" I asked.

"The one that started it, he's been locked up in the hospital," said the waiter. "He must be bloody crazy." He said that the man had gone berserk and had tried to hit anyone who got in his way. One of the crew had picked up the screaming man and dragged him to the hospital, where the man tried to attack the doctor. The crew member threw him against the bulkhead and knocked him out. The waiter said that the other Indians were running around saying that they'd get their friend out of the hospital if they had to sink the ship to do it. The captain had stationed guards at the hospital and was calling the Singapore police to have them pick up the Indians when we docked.

The hospital was aft of the bar, on the same deck. We went outside. The deck was deserted except for two crew members from the engine room who were standing by the entrance to the hospital. As we stood by the rail, the smaller of the other two Indians came up from below and walked over to one of the guards. He talked to him for a moment, and the guard smiled and shook his head. Then the Indian began to wave his arms, and the guard laughed. The Indian screamed, "We'll get him out, you'll see! We'll get him out!" He walked away from the hospital toward us. He was thin, and had very dark, deep-set eyes. There was almost no white showing, and his pupils, we could see from a few feet away, were huge. Suddenly he stopped and turned back toward the guard. "God damned white men!" he shrieked. "White bastards! We'll get you all when we get to Singapore. God damned white men! God damned white men!" He turned, shouting obscenities, and ran down the stairs.

Later that afternoon, I was sitting in one of the lounges when a girl I had met at a dance the night before came over and sat beside me. She was one of the loveliest women I'd ever seen—a tall, slim Indian with smooth black hair, dark eyes, and sharp features. Her skin was a rich honey tan. She had told me that her husband could not get a vacation that year and had sent her on a cruise to Japan. She was traveling with a group of friends.

"I just wanted to say that after what happened today, I am ashamed for my people," she said.

"It was a pity," I said.

"I am afraid that people will judge all Indians by those few bad ones, and that is unjust. We ourselves hate them. They have caused trouble all the way. They have forced some of their countrymen to give them money."

"Why didn't you tell the captain?"

"He would not have cared. He would have said that it was our problem."

"How do you know that?"

"I know." She paused. "You do not hold this against all Indians, do you?"

"No, of course not."

"I am glad. The crew does. I heard them before, two of them on deck. They were using the old talk, referring to us as bloody wogs. They said we should all be thrown overboard."

"They were just talking."

"I know, but they feel it. They do not like Indians. Any Indians."

"During the trouble today," I said, "one of the men tried to get his friend loose, and when he couldn't, he got flustered and started screaming about white men in general. That fascinated me. I wondered why he chose that as his last defense. Why did that particular feeling of inferiority come out? He isn't any darker than most white men."

"Why did that come out? Because he has felt all his life that the white men consider him inferior. We all feel this, because it is true. For years we have been put down by the white men—by the British, by everybody. It is a natural reaction."

"You mean you think you've been kept down because of your skin color? In India, where skin colors vary from as white as me to as dark as an African Negro?"

"Yes. Some people say it is nationality, not color. But that is not true. The colored man has always been considered inferior. Why do you consider colored people inferior?"

"Me! How did I get into this? What makes you think I consider colored people inferior?"

"I'm sure you do. Let me ask you this. Would you marry a colored woman?"

"What do you mean by colored woman? Any woman whose skin isn't white?"

"Yes."

"Are you a colored woman?"

"Yes."

"Then yes, I would."

She was embarrassed, but she wanted to press her point. "Then would you marry a Negress?"

"If I were in love with her."

"That is hedging. Could you fall in love with a Negress?"

"Probably not."

"Why not?"

"Partly because of the way I was brought up. But it isn't purely a matter of color distinction, or anything quite so simple as that. It's a matter of cultural differences, of differences in background and opportunity, the same differences that would make it difficult for a Negress to find *me* attractive. Also, such a marriage would involve innumerable difficulties on both sides. The problems we as a couple would encounter in everyday life would probably make both of us hold back."

"Now there is what I mean," she said. "The problems. Forgetting for a moment you as an individual, why does your country have such a prejudice against colored people?"

"There's no simple answer. But you have a prejudice here that is somewhat the same. Look at the difficulties you would encounter if you married an Untouchable. India has age-old class prejudices. The prejudice in the United States is against the Negroes. Thirty or forty years ago, it was against Jews."

"Would I be discriminated against in your country?"

"Probably not, no."

"What do you mean, 'probably not.' Can you not give me a yes or no answer?"

I was ashamed, but I felt I had to tell her what I knew to be the truth. "You would not be discriminated against," I said, "if you wore Indian clothes."

"Oh, so now it is a clothes prejudice. You mean if I wore a blouse and a skirt, European clothes, I would be considered black. If I wore a sari, I would be considered white. Or not white, perhaps, but at least not colored. I could go anywhere, eat with anyone, sleep in any hotel."

"I'm afraid so."

"And you wondered," she said slowly, "why that man this morning cursed you white men?"

15

In Thailand, the subtitles on English-language films run down the right side of the screen. Charlie and I were watching pretty Natalie Wood and robust Warren Beatty pour out their supposedly teen-age souls over social taboos and the problems of adolescent sexuality, and every teary, halting word was written on the side of the screen in floral Siamese script. We had not intended to go to an American movie our first night in Bangkok, since this hardly seemed the best way to see a new city, but circumstance after circumstance had driven us toward the gaudy modern theater and *Splendor in the Grass*.

We arrived late in the afternoon from Kuala Lumpur, Malaya, aboard Royal Thai Airlines. In Kuala Lumpur, where we had gone after two uneventful days in Singapore

(called by all airline crews "the poor man's Hong Kong"),
we had been taken under the wing of my godfather, a bright,
dedicated, charming man named Harry Casler who works
for USIS. The city itself, the capital of Malaya, is modern,
prosperous, and beautiful, a sort of lively and tasteful Brasilia
growing in the middle of the Malayan jungle. It was a curious sensation to leave a cocktail party in the most modern
of houses and be advised not to stray off the paved roads and
into the jungle for fear of pythons and elephants. At first,
we were skeptical of the warning, convinced that this was the
standard ribbing given to newcomers to Kuala Lumpur.
Then one morning I leafed through a copy of the Malaya
Straits Times, and found the following article:

ELEPHANT WRECKS CAR
HOUR AFTER IT'S BOUGHT

Ipoh, Wed.—Inche Noordin bin Shaari, 24, will never forget the night he met an elephant on the road to Grik.

Mainly because the truculent tusker ("It was huge")
charged and damaged his pride and joy—a brand new 4500
dollar car delivered to him a few hours earlier.

The elephant evidently knew the location of its wheeled
adversary's "heart," for it concentrated its attack on the
vehicle's bonnet, plunging a tusk through it and bashing it
in with a flailing trunk.

Inche Noordin, an assistant rural industries officer at
Kuala Lipis, told his story today:

It began early on Monday when he went to Kuala Lumpur with a 4500 dollar government cheque, paid it to a
motor firm and took delivery of a new Morris Minor 1,000.

"I was anxious to drive to Grik to show my parents the
car," he said.

"However, my friend—and my girl friend—advised me to

spend the night either in Ipoh or in Kuala Kangsar. I reached Kuala Kangsar at about 6 p.m. intending to spend the night there at my sister's. But my eagerness to get home was too strong.

"So I set off again. I was about ten miles from Grik at about 10:30 p.m. when I saw a huge elephant standing in the middle of the road.

"I stopped and after a few minutes switched off my headlights hoping it would go away. After ten minutes I turned the lights on again.

"The brute was still there. Suddenly it trumpeted loudly and charged."

Inche Noordin hastily abandoned the car and ran to a nearby kampong for help.

When he returned with villagers armed with shotguns and lights the elephant had finished savaging the car and gone— leaving a trail of 18-inch prints in the road.

TRUNK NOTE: When Inche Noordin finally reached Grik at 4 a.m. it was to find that has father had gone to Kroh, a town several miles away on the Malaya-Thailand border.

We had not reserved a room in Bangkok, and so when we arrived at the airport, we began making the tedious inquiries as to what was available, how much it cost, and how close to the center of town it was. One of the airline personnel handed us a bunch of cards on which were written the names and addresses of hotels. We picked one at random, a red card with the name "Saha Kit" and an address that we were told was within walking distance of the center of Bangkok, hailed a rickshaw taxi, and started off.

The Hotel Saha Kit admirably fulfilled one of our demands: it was cheap. Clean, it wasn't. Comfortable, it never had been, not the day it was built. For the amenities of a regular hotel (a bar, a restaurant, and privacy), it substituted an attraction not uncommon to hotels all over the world, but seldom so blatantly displayed: a flophouse, the Saha Kit was a cathouse as well. As soon as the manager had ascertained that we were not from Interpol or some international vice squad, he made it clear to us that we could commandeer any number of young ladies. When we declined, he got suspicious again, and was surly and unpleasant as he showed us to what served as our room.

The room was no more than eight feet wide and fifteen feet long. Somehow, probably by building the room around the furniture, the management had squeezed in two beds end to end. At one end of the room, by the narrow window that looked out on a courtyard crisscrossed with sagging laundry lines, was an open stall that contained a cold-water-only basin, a cold-water-only shower, and a commode that functioned when and if it chose to. At the other end of the room was the door, the bottom half wood and the top half wire screening, which afforded neither privacy nor silence at any time of the day.

Like many hotels that cater to more than one animal need, the Saha Kit ran on a two- to three-shift, twenty-four hour basis. Some people rented rooms from eight in the morning until four in the afternoon, some from four to twelve, and some from twelve to eight. Some people rented rooms for half an hour. Families of four and more lived in double rooms: the father worked from six in the morning till six at night, the children from four in the afternoon till midnight, and the mother at all odd hours, so somebody was always awake making noise. Those that were fortunate enough to work only a ten-hour day, usually late into the night, partied and chattered and fought until the early morning, when they shoved somebody to the other side of a bed and climbed in for a few hours rest.

Women in dressing gowns padded up and down the halls at all hours of the day and night, giggling at the gooses of groping customers. I had lain down for a few minutes nap as soon as we had paid the manager in advance for one night, but sleep, I soon discovered, was impossible. Passers-by stopped at our door and pushed their noses flat against the wire screen and giggled and yelled and banged on the door.

At seven o'clock in the evening Charlie and I fled, desperate to find something to do that would keep us away from the Saha Kit until we became so tired that we could sleep through the chaos. We had dinner, and then walked around the city in search of entertainment. But we didn't want to go to a nightclub, and the only other entertainment that seemed to be available was expensive and perhaps diseased. So when we saw the marquee for *Splendor in the Grass*, we darted inside, more to escape from the passion merchants than to see a movie, and spent two glorious hours dramatically involved with other people's problems.

Some cities, like Paris and Rome and Hong Kong, are havens for all kinds of travelers. There are sights to see, and when the sights have been seen, one can live a fascinating, entertaining existence just walking around the city, eating in the myriad restaurants, going to the theater, sitting in the *piazzas* and *parcs* or on the hills overlooking the sea, and poking around the shops that sell everything from Chinese sculpture to medieval firearms. Bangkok is a city for tourists and silk and jewel buyers only. There are about two days worth of sights to see—the klongs, or canals, the Temple of

the Dawn, the gold Buddha, the palace, and the other temples which, to the eye untrained in Thai art, look very much
alike—and there are two superb silk stores—one, Star of
Siam, in a hotel, and the other, Thai Silk Co., Ltd., owned
by an American named Jim Thompson. The good hotels are
frightfully expensive, and the others, like the Saha Kit, do
not encourage long stays. Aside from the dollar-and-a-half-a-
drink spectaculars at the big hotels, there is no night life for
foreigners.

When we had seen the sights and bought silk to send home,
Charlie and I were ready to leave. We knew no one in Bangkok, and knowing people is the only thing that makes cities
like Bangkok and Teheran bearable for more than two days.
We stayed one extra day to see some Thai boxing matches.
Thai boxing utilizes both the hands and feet, and some of
the most severe blows are delivered by knees to the kidney
and feet to the head. We sat through six matches in the
crowded arena, listening to the frantic shouts of bettors all
around us and the whining ritual music played all through
the fights. The first five fights were draws or decisions, patty-
cake matches by young fighters who kicked and swung wildly
and with little grace. The sixth fight, the main event, ended
when the man in red trunks kicked the man in blue trunks
in the temple and knocked him flying through the air to
come down on the canvas with a thud like a sandbag dropped
on a wooden floor. The man in blue trunks lay crumpled
on the floor until his trainers carried him out of the ring.
Not once did he stir or open an eye as they put him on a
stretcher and took him from the arena.

As we waited to board the plane for Hong Kong, I spied a
thin, elderly lady, whom I recognized as a friend of a friend,
coming down the ramp from a plane that had just landed.

I went over and introduced myself to her as she stood in line for customs inspection. She said that she had recently lost her husband, and since she had nothing to keep her home, she was taking a trip around the world.

"But darling, it's so *expen*sive!" she said. "All this traveling first class."

"You could go tourist," I said.

"I would have, darling, but I *couldn't,* not with four suitcases. The overweight charge would have been fantastic."

"Four suitcases! Why do you need four suitcases? Are you going to a ball every night?"

"It's not *clothes,* for pity sakes. Who needs that many clothes?"

"Not clothes?"

"Metrecal, darling. Two suitcases of Metrecal and two of clothes, all wash and wear. Very practical, don't you think?"

"Metrecal!" I said. "It's a curious time to go on a diet."

"Oh, but I'm not on a diet. I was told, by people who ought to know, that one just *can't* eat the food in India. So I decided not to take any chances."

If you have heard nothing else about Hong Kong, you have heard about its tailors. You have seen friends come home from Hong Kong with beautiful English suits and heard them say, with forced casualness, "Oh, this thing? This was only thirty-five dollars. Custom made, of course. Silk lining." You have read about how you are greeted at the airport, in the cab, on the bus, in the lobby of your hotel, and finally in your room by little men with tape measures, and about how tailors are the first and last people you see every day. They have a reputation for being the fastest (they arrive in your room, if not before you, at least before the man who is following you with your baggage), the most persistent (phone calls, letters in your mailbox, ads slipped under your door), and the most persuasive (no one ever spends more than twenty-four hours in Hong Kong without leaving with at least two suits and five shirts) merchants in the world.

The reputation is deserved, but it is incomplete. They *are* the fastest, the most persistent, and the most persuasive, but they are in mortal competition with another group of merchants who are but a wink behind them and may soon overtake them. The tailors are running neck and neck with the procurers, and if it were not for the tailors' determined spurt at the finish line, they would long since have disappeared from first place. Just as everyone knows the name of the heavyweight champion of the world but has no idea who the top contender is, so everyone has heard of the tailors but knows nothing of their pursuers.

The pimps are at one disadvantage: they have less experience in daytime fighting than the tailors. By tradition they are night fighters, when skulking rather than running is the necessary talent, and their ranks are as yet not deep enough in good sprinters. Regardless, they perform admirably.

Charlie and I arrived in Hong Kong at five in the afternoon. As we stood in the customs area, we could see crowds of men in dark suits clustering around the exit gate, and we were grateful for time to prepare ourselves in the quiet of government sanctuary for the onslaught ahead. We did not realize that the rank and file of government employees could be infiltrated.

I was standing next to my suitcase, waiting for the man to come and put the chalk mark on it so I could pass. He

opened the bag of a woman standing next to me, asked her
if she had anything to declare, closed her bag, marked it, and
came to me.

"Anything to declare?" he asked.

"No."

"American?"

"Yes."

He took up his pad and made believe he was writing something on it. "You like nice girl?" he whispered.

"No, thank you."

"Real nice girl. English schoolteacher."

"No, thank you."

"Sure? Any size, shape, color you like. Real nice girl."

"If they're so nice, what are they doing in this business?"

He hesitated. "Okay, Joe," he said, and he scribbled the
pass mark on my bag.

We had just arrived in our room and had lain down for
a moment before unpacking, when there was a hard bump-
ing against our door, followed by a few sharp words in Chinese and then a quick knock. I got up and opened the door.
A Chinese in a well-cut black suit stood in the doorway with
a briefcase.

"May I come in?" he said.

"Sure," I said. "What was all the racket?"

"Oh, that. It was nothing."

I let him in and then looked down the hall. The room boy
was sitting disconsolately on his little stool at the end of the
hall. When he saw me, he gave me a broad smile and a wave.
I went back to the room and shut the door.

The man was already working on Charlie. "I am the hotel
tailor," he said. "Private representative, guaranteed by the
hotel. I would like to take your orders."

"Take our orders!" said Charlie. "How do you know we want anything?"

The man looked astounded. "You mean you are not going to have a suit made? In *Hong Kong?*"

"We haven't decided. And even if we do, maybe we won't want to use you as a tailor. Maybe we want to look around."

"Of course, of course. But you will not find a better tailor than Harold Kwang, of that you can be sure."

"I'm sure," said Charlie. "When we decide, we'll let you know."

"How long are you staying in Hong Kong?"

"A week. Maybe ten days."

"I would advise you to order now. The more time we have, the more fittings we can arrange. Also, you can buy more suits if you like the first one."

"I think we'll wait and see," said Charlie.

"I will call you tomorrow and see if you have decided."

"No, don't call us. We'll call you if we want anything."

"As you wish. But when you decide, you can get me direct through my hotel extension, 100. Here is my card." He bowed and went out.

I didn't even have time to lie down again before there was a knock on the door. I opened it, and the room boy stood there, holding a pitcher of water.

"I bring you water," he said.

"Okay. You can set it over there."

I left the door open while he set the water down. He came back, and I held the door for him. "Thanks," I said.

"No," he said. He moved me away from the door and shut it firmly. "You like nice girl?"

"No, thanks."

"Very cheap, too. Any kind you like." He moved his

hands four ways, for short girl, tall girl, fat girl, and thin girl.

"Do you want one, Charlie?"

Charlie shook his head. "Thanks anyway, but not at six o'clock in the afternoon."

"Good time for diddly," said the boy.

"No," I said, "not good time for diddly."

"Ah, yes. Sun just goin' down. Very good time for . . ." He made a circle with two fingers and moved the index finger of the other hand back and forth through it.

"Thanks anyway, but I don't think so. We'll call you if we need you."

"Okay, you lose." He started to go out.

"Hey, by the way," I said. "Did you and that tailor arrive at our door at the same time?"

"Yes," he said.

"Why did you let him beat you in?"

"He say he tell manager on me if I don' let him in 'fore me." He turned and went out.

As far as we were concerned, the contest was even now at one round apiece. That night, the pimps took a decisive lead. Some of the tailor shops stay open at night, but just as six in the afternoon is not the perfect time for purchasing "diddly," so at eleven at night few people are interested in buying suits.

We were set upon four times in one block. Once in the hotel lobby, once in front of a nightclub, once in front of a drugstore, and once in front of a movie theater. The one in front of the movie theater had just finished his course in persistence.

When we had gone through the "You like nice girl?" pitch, he started on a new one. "Maybe you like boys?" This was an intelligent ploy: if it was true, he had a sale, and if it was not, he figured he could insult us into proving our virility. But it didn't work.

"No," I said, which left him no avenue of attack short of being boisterously insulting, which he was not about to do. Honor of the trade, no doubt.

"You like see some dirty pictures? Four movies. Hot stuff."

"No."

We were walking, and he scurried along to keep up with us. "Two movies half price."

"No."

"How 'bout show? I got it real. Two girls do it, boy girl do it. Right front of you. You sit watch. They do anything you like. You the boss. You tell 'em, they do."

"You have a large inventory," I said, "but no thanks."

He had run out of goods, and, disgusted, he walked away.

Perhaps the Hong Kong pimps will never get the recognition they deserve. True, their wares are to be found all over the world, and their prices are not remarkably low. Yet these people have great talent and great color, much more than the tailors, who already have a huge market and are only trying to take business away from one another. The pimps are continually concocting new sales techniques and offering new pleasures, working to expand their clientele.

Being in Hong Kong was like being back in Europe, and for a week Charlie and I luxuriated in the cosmopolitan, vibrant atmosphere of the great city. We stayed in three hotels, from the austere (cheap and clean) YMCA to the middle-priced, plastic-furniture Shamrock, to the plush Miramar. We were fitted for suits at Maiwo Yang, for shirts at Mee Yee, and for shoes at Lee Kee. We sat on straw mats and drank bird's-nest soup and ate sweet and sour pork. We danced with two Pan American stewardesses to "Mountain Greenery" at a top-floor restaurant that overlooked the whole colony. We rode the Star Ferry from Kowloon to Hong Kong and back, drinking English gin and Scotch whisky from paper cups. We twisted with ladies of the evening in waterfront bars on the island of Hong Kong. We talked politics with a British shipper and a Chinese law student. We walked through the snake market at two in the morning and saw Chinese housewives carefully choosing the long, writhing serpents that would feed their families the next day. When a woman made a choice, the stallkeeper picked the snake out of the cage, made a small incision, and skinned it in an instant. The snake was still twitching as the man wrapped it in newspaper and dropped it in the woman's shopping bag.

We could have spent another two weeks in Hong Kong without being bored, snooping around the narrow streets, window-shopping, meeting people, touring deep in the New Territories on the Red Chinese border. But every day the itch to get home grew stronger. It had first become noticeable in India, where the heat and discomfort and boredom of Ahmedabad and Bombay had made us long for the comfort and activity of home, and it had gotten worse when we passed the halfway mark and began what was, technically, the home stretch. At first, we had both been conscientious about seeing everything and meeting everyone, and even as far east as Bangkok we were still taking advantage of all our contacts. In Bankok, we had tried to make arrangements to go to Angkor Wat, in Cambodia, the fabulous ruins which everyone had said we should see. But it was difficult to acquire the necessary visas and get plane reservations on the irregular and uncertain run between Thailand and Cambodia, and the trip would have cost us an extra week and a considerable amount of money. Six weeks earlier, we would have taken the trip and written off the time and expense to education. As it was, we had decided not to go.

So when we picked up our Hong Kong suits and shirts and shoes, we spent one last night on the town and, on the 18th of April, flew to Tokyo.

16

IN JAPAN, our blasé approach to the problem of reservations finally caught up with us—with a vengeance. We arrived in Tokyo at midnight, in the teeth of an unseasonal downpour, and were curtly informed that there was not a room to be had anywhere in the city.

"It is Golden Week, you know," said a stiffly formal Japanese. "Cherry blossom time. People come from all over the world for Golden Week."

Accompanied by ten or twelve other people who had neglected to make reservations, we waited in the Pan American office until one-thirty while a tired, beleaguered clerk called every hotel in Tokyo and pleaded for rooms. In vain. We hailed a taxi and told the driver to take us to a hotel. He laughed. At quarter to three, after trying fourteen hotels and running up a $7 taxi bill, we were condescendingly accepted at a hotel and assigned to a three-room suite, for which we paid $22—in advance.

"Only for tonight, sir," said the clerk. "The room is reserved for tomorrow. Checkout time is ten-thirty."

The next morning, we went to the desk and started calling hotels. Four of the first five we called said flatly no. The fifth said they would put us on a list, and that we might be able to get a room sometime around the end of the month.

"How about Japanese inns?" I asked the clerk. "Would any of them have rooms?" We had wanted to stay in a Japanese inn to begin with, but they were not listed in the phone book.

"Japanese *inns?*" said the clerk. "In Tokyo? Tell me, are there any colonial inns in New York City?" So much for Japanese inns.

Finally, we found a hotel that would have us ("Of course, you will have to stay in the unrenovated wing"), and although it was twice as expensive as we could comfortably afford, we accepted eagerly. When we had unpacked, we hurried to American Express to make reservations to go to Kyoto and Nara. We definitely wanted to stay in a Japanese inn in Kyoto, and we wanted to make sure that we had a reservation.

"Are you serious?" said the man at American Express.

"Why, yes," I said.

"Well, I'll try," he said, "but you have about as much chance as if you'd asked me to move the emperor out of his palace and give you his bedroom."

An hour later, he had an answer. "No," he said. "But there's always a chance that you could get something if you just showed up there. A cancellation or something."

"And if we can't?" said Charlie.

"Then you come back to Tokyo. Unless you want to sleep in the street." We were debating whether or not to take the chance, when the man said, "I can get you plane reservations to Kyoto, but I think you should know that it will cost the two of you about a hundred and twenty dollars round trip."

"We're going to get home sooner than we thought," said Charlie.

We thanked the man for his time. We went back to the hotel and tried to decide how to spend our glorious, fun-filled week in sprawling Tokyo, the biggest city in the world. We were unable to find our way around, for the streets are neither numbered nor named (in *any* language). We didn't speak the language, so every time we went out we had to ask the concierge to write on a piece of paper in Japanese where we wanted to go; when we got lost, we showed the paper to a passerby, who usually shrugged his shoulders or pointed vaguely in any direction that came to mind.

A Japanese friend we looked up decided that as part of our education we should go to a Japanese bath. He said he realized that most Americans have heard wild stories about the Japanese baths, and he thought we should see for ourselves what they were like.

To the Japanese the public baths are, very simply, a part of their daily life, and those who can afford it (for they are not cheap) stop in often on their way home from work. It must have been the occupation forces who first awakened the American mind to Japanese baths, and stirred it with tales of free love. Like hotels, there are respectable baths and not-so-respectable baths, the latter being more brothels-with-a-gimmick than places to bathe oneself. Regardless, what is to the Japanese a daily ritual has become to American tourists a source of curiosity and amusement, and Charlie and I were anxious to test the myth firsthand.

At five-thirty one afternoon, Charlie and I, led by our friend, entered a four-story building, outside of which hung three neon signs in Japanese. They were translated for us as saying, "Finnish sauna baths," "Individual Turkish baths," and "Group baths." We climbed to the second floor, where the ticket office was, and our escort bought three tickets.

"What kind are these for?" asked Charlie as we walked to the waiting room.

"Individual," said the man.

We sat in the lounge for perhaps five minutes, when three young women came in, two from a corridor that ran off the lounge to the right, one from a corridor on the left. Two of the three women were small and round, like fat lady gnomes. The third was tall and husky. The two little ones headed for the Japanese man and myself. They took our hands and led us off down the corridor on the right. As we left the room, my chubby little filly and I, I glanced back and saw Charlie being marched down the other corridor by the big one. He walked rather stiffly, I thought, not with the determined gait I knew to be the real Ravenel.

My girl was clothed in a loose-fitting white bathrobe, and as soon as she led me into a small anteroom, containing only a massage table, and closed the door behind us, she shed her bathrobe, revealing a pair of white panties and a white bra.

She knelt down and took off my shoes. She went around behind me and peeled off my jacket, then motioned for me to take off my tie and shirt, which I managed to do. Then she waved her hand at me and said, "All," and walked into the bathroom. Gingerly, I took off my socks and threw them over my jacket. Then I stood there, unsure of what to do next. The girl came back into the room, and when she saw that I still had my pants on, she said "Tch-tch," undid my belt, removed my trousers, and hung them up. "Off," she said, pointing to my shorts. After a moment's hesitation, I pulled down my shorts and stepped out of them. "Good," she said, and clapped her hands. She smiled broadly, and I saw that her two front teeth were black.

When I had spent ten minutes enclosed up to my chin in a steam cabinet, the girl said "Out," and pointed to a stool not much bigger around than a salad plate. I sat down on it, and she picked up a bucket of almost scalding water and threw it over me. I leapt to my feet, but she pushed me down again and began to rub me with a bar of soap. When the soaping was done, she jammed me into the tiny tub, where I lay half submerged in steaming-hot water for about a minute, with both legs sticking full length over the end. The girl laughed at my position and said, "Beeeg mahn."

When she had dried me with a bath towel, she shoved me face down onto the massage table. She began at the calf of one leg and worked up to the thigh, then down the other leg, slapping me first with the back of her hand, then with her palm. After the slapping, she worked on my back with her elbows, digging in and moving her arms in small circles.

"Did you learn this one from de Sade?" I said, groaning as her elbows burrowed into my back.

"Wha' say?"

"Forget it."

She stopped for a moment and I thought the ordeal was over. I began to sit up. "No," she said, and she hoisted herself onto the table.

"Now wait a minute," I said, but it was too late. She

placed one foot on my right thigh, the other on my left, and
began to walk up my back. I had heard tales of petites
masseuses running up and down your back, but this girl
was anything but petite. I felt as if a hefty Landrace sow
with feet like Primo Carnera was trying a primeval *bossa
nova* on my back.

"Okay?" she asked politely. I groaned, and counted myself lucky as I remembered that Charlie's girl was bigger than
he.

"You're some lot of broad to be doing the 440 on my
vertebrae," I said.

"Wha' say, Joe?" she said.

"Oh, God!"

She jumped off the table, turned me over, and repeated the
whole process on my front, slapping the thighs, digging the
elbows into my sternum, walking on my stomach. Then she
grabbed my left hand and wrenched thumb and little finger
in opposite directions. There was a sharp crack. The girl
giggled. She took the three middle fingers and crunched
them together, then yanked them apart. Another crack.
She reached for my right hand. "Oh, no, you don't," I said.

She laughed, and said, "Okay, Joe." She grabbed my ears
and pulled me into a sitting position.

As I dressed, I moved my limbs to see if anything was
broken. Everything seemed to be in order, and to my
surprise, I felt relaxed and well.

"School?" said the girl.

"Teacher," I said.

"Smoke?"

"Fire."

The girl laughed. "American?"

"Flag."

The girl looked at a clock on the wall, said *arigato,* and pushed me out the door.

We spent the next few days running between Tokyo University and America House, an academic institution for Americans in Tokyo and for Japanese who want to study about America. We talked to teachers and students, business men and politicians, and we noticed that in all our conversations one subject came up again and again: the reasons behind the riots that forced President Eisenhower to cancel his trip to Japan in 1960. Though the subject was always the same, the way it was brought up varied, depending on whom we were talking to—sometimes it was mentioned in a tone of humble apology, sometimes in a tone of angry defense. Our last day in Japan, we asked a man who was working with America House why the Japanese felt compelled to dwell on this unfortunate incident.

"With some people, it's a feeling of guilt," said the man. "They want you to believe that the riots are not indicative of how the people of Japan feel toward America. With others, it's just the opposite. They want to impress upon you Japan's independence, her unwillingness to submit to any one nation. They want to get all foreigners out of Japan, and they hate the idea of any alliance that demands something from them. That's one of the main troubles with Japanese society today—it's riddled with this sort of conflict."

The roots of these conflicts, he said, lay in the defeat in 1945 and the subsequent shakeup of the old, formal, highly stratified society. For hundreds of years, the Japanese people had nothing to do with the outside world. The average Japanese man took no part in the governing of his country, and his whole life revolved around local and family affairs, which were controlled by a strong ethic designed only for small groups. The Japanese were never taught to think in terms of "democracy" or "liberty," but in terms of "honor" and "duty." So "government" per se was an alien concept.

They did not choose their present form of government— it was set upon them after the war. Similarly, they did not choose to be allied with the Western bloc. They just happened to have been conquered by its strongest member. But the government and the alliance served Japan well for the first few years after the war. The country was financed and defended, which left Japan unconcerned with anything but the construction of a solid economic basis for its society.

It is only in recent years, since Japan has become strong on its own, that it has begun to demand a say in its national and international affairs. And the more demands the Japanese achieved, the more power they had; and the more power they had, the more demands they made.

To a certain extent, the conflict in Japanese society is between generations. The older generation, deeply loyal to Japanese tradition and ethic, is cautious, concerned with the safety of Japan and willing to wait and decide which side will be the winner before committing itself. The younger generation, which has no solid background of tradition, and which is beset by fears of war and weakened by lack of knowledge about the world, chases new ideas with the fervor of a dog chasing rabbits. While they are in school, Japanese youths are taught by some Marxist professors, and they hear from the powerful Teachers' Union that ". . . peace is what the people want, but the capitalists do not make money from peace, and so they see it as a terrible threat to them." These words and others, such as "imperialistic warmongers," make the students, who are pitifully uninformed about the Communist countries, easy prey for the left-wing Zengakuren, the Communists, and other militant groups.

Japanese neutralism is motivated by two qualities: cynicism and terror. The Japanese want to be defended, but they don't want to defend themselves. They are afraid of a nuclear war, and while they want to have some voice in preventing it, they don't want to align themselves with either side for fear of upsetting the balance of power.

"Japan's is an awkward position," said the man from America House. "She doesn't want us to think she's going communistic, because she's not. She doesn't want the Communists to think she's going to the West, because she's not. So she ends up by appearing to have no ideology at all, except neutrality. The sad part is that she *doesn't* have any clear-cut ideology. And perhaps it would be unrealistic to ask that she did."

17

GOOD AFTERNOON," said the voice over the loudspeaker. "This is your captain speaking. Our landing in Honolulu will be delayed approximately twenty minutes. A military convoy is taking off, and we have to wait until they're clear of the field."

"Oh, swell," I said. "Now I suppose he'll run out of gas." I could practically hear the strains of "The High and the Mighty."

"Have another drink," said Charlie. He yawned and closed his eyes.

The plane leveled off and flew straight for two or three minutes. Then suddenly the nose dropped, a little at first, then more, then still more, until it was perhaps twenty degrees off level. I heard a crash, and three trays flew down the aisle and clattered against the barrier between first class and tourist. A woman across the aisle from me dropped her purse. It snapped open, and a lipstick and rouge and coins and keys rolled forward.

"Hi, there!" said the voice on the loudspeaker. "This is your captain again. For those of you who haven't flown Pan American Jet Clipper Service before, I'd like to say that this is not a normal landing procedure. We're descending at approximately four thousand feet a minute. By the way," he added, "in case you think we're going a little fast, I'd like to say that we've got all the garbage possible out there on the wings to slow us down."

I tried to grip the arms of the seat, but my hands were so sweaty they kept slipping off. I nudged Charlie. "Hey, did you hear that? Four thousand feet a minute."

"Good," he said, sleepily. "That must mean we're almost there."

For the first few hours in Honolulu, Charlie and I didn't fully realize that we were back in the United States. We took a room at the YMCA, which is like the Hong Kong YMCA only slightly more elaborate, and we walked around the city, as we had done in every city we visited. Then we decided to get something to eat.

"What'll it be, Jack?" said the pock-marked young man in the soiled waiter's jacket.

"Two cheeseburgers and a Coke," I said.

"Same for me," said Charlie. "Only, no cheese."

"Have you got enough money?" I asked Charlie.

"I better have. I've got two or three bucks."

We ate our food, and asked for the bill. "Two-ninety!" said Charlie. "Two-ninety for what?"

The young man looked at his pad. "For two Steerburgers, two Special Cheese Supremes, and two Cokes, that's what," he said.

Charlie left three dollars on the table, and we stood up. "Thanks, big-timer," said the waiter.

We knew we were home. Taxis started at fifty cents and jumped a dime every fifth or sixth of a mile. Movies cost a dollar or a dollar and a half. Shirts cost twenty-five or thirty cents each to launder. And we couldn't get an edible meal for less than four dollars apiece. It was the wrong place for us.

The next morning, we went to Waikiki. Waikiki is a long, curved beach in a shallow cove. At one end of the beach is a huge pink hotel. At the other end is Diamond Head. Between the two sprawls an unbroken line of hotels— white hotels, blue hotels, yellow hotels, pink hotels, hotels named Princess Kaiulani and Moana and Hilton Hawaiian Village. The hotels do not go all the way up to Diamond Head—yet. But trees have been cut down and land cleared, and within five years the whole beach will probably be one sprawling hotelopolis.

Charlie and I walked to the shore on a narrow path between two hotels. At the beginning of the path was a sign, "Private walk—for hotels guests only," but no one stopped us. We spread towels on the crowded beach and rushed toward the water. On my first step into the water I opened the sole of my left foot on a piece of coral. On my second step I twisted my ankle on a rock and fell forward on my face in two feet of water. We found that the only safe way to get to deeper water was to sit with our hands under us and slowly propel ourselves with our hands until we reached swimming depth. As I worked my way away from the beach, scuttling across the coral like a deformed crab, a man who was floating in a chartreuse inner tube called to me. "Hey, bud," he said, "watcha doing?"

I settled down gently in the water and looked at him. He was fat and extraordinarily hairy. He had hair on his stomach, his chest, his shoulders, his back, his neck, his legs and his toes, and hair sprouted from his ears and nose like tufts of grass. He carried two cigars stuffed into the elastic of his bathing suit. "I am trying to get to less dangerous waters," I said.

"Should have got yourself an inner tube," he said. "If you sit right, it saves your ass, too."

"It's a little late to think of that. I'm at the point of no return. I might as well keep going."

"Why don't you tell the old lady to throw you a tube?"

"There is no old lady. If I had a wife, you can bet your life I wouldn't be here."

"No wife? Now there is a lucky man. Bud, I wisht I was in your shoes. Some of the ginch on this here island is well worth the trouble. But not with a wife. No sir. I'd never bring my wife here again. I'll come alone next time."

"Does your wife enjoy it here?" I said.

"Sure. She enjoys any place she can get away with spending a hundred bucks a day. Don't matter for what. Right now she's having a *hula* lesson, fa crissakes! She should do the hula like I should do a goddam ballet dance. An American beauty rose is one thing she ain't."

"And what about you? Do you like it here?"

"You know what this is? Atlantic City with palm trees. Sure, it's all right. It's warm, and I get a tan. It's a change from Miami, anyway."

"Well, nice to meet you," I said. I pushed myself forward on my hands.

"Yeah," he said. "Don't forget to get an inner tube."

I spent the afternoon skinning my chest and swallowing salt water in a grotesque attempt at surfboarding. I gave that up as a bad job when the board got away from me and narrowly missed decapitating a young girl. I returned the surfboard to the rental booth and bought a sandwich and a Coke with the dollar and a half I had planned to spend renting the surfboard for another hour.

The next night, after spending ten hours on the beach, we decided to leave Honolulu and go to some of the outlying islands, reportedly less developed and less expensive. In principle, it was a splendid idea. In practice it turned out that transportation to the other islands was more expensive than two days' room and board in Honolulu.

Four hours later, when my system had given up trying to adapt itself to the three zombies I had had at Don the Beachcomber's and was letting balance, reason, and digestion go their own detached ways, I bought six rolls of nickels, shut myself in a phone booth, and gave the long distance operator a number in Alexandria, Virginia.

"Hello," said the voice of my lost lady love.

"That will be ten dollars and forty cents for the first three minutes," said the operator. I started pumping nickels into the machine, and I could hear laughter on the other end.

"There!" I said, triumphantly. "Hi!"

"I knew it was you."

"I knew you'd knew—you'd know. Anyway, I knew it, too. Hey, are you free for dinner tomorrow night?"

"Yes," she said. "Where are you?"

"I'm not altogether certain," I said. "The last time I had any conscious knowledge of anything, I was in Hawaii. Right now it's anybody's guess."

"Hawaii!"

"Hawaii. I'll see you tomorrow afternoon. I'll call you from the airport. Farewell." I hung up.

I went upstairs and packed.

"Well, *I'm* going to the Seattle fair," said Charlie when I told him of my dinner engagement.

"Enjoy yourself," I said. "I just can't see going all the way up there for a fair. A circus, maybe. A fair, no. When do you leave?"

"I think I'll leave tonight, too," he said. "I'm not all that sure *why* I'm going to the fair, but I'm going. All there'll be are exhibits from the countries we've just seen. There won't be anything new."

"There won't be anything new," I repeated. I stood up as straight as my inner ear would permit, raised one eyebrow, and said in a most sententious tone, "Beware. This same philosophy is a good horse in the stable, but an arrant jade on a journey."

"Come on," said Charlie. "Let's get to the airport before you fall down and hurt yourself." As he led me out of the room, he mumbled, " 'An arrant jade on a journey.' What are you, some kind of nut?"